How Christians Behave

How Christians Behave

The Foundation Series
Volume Two

by

Kenneth N. Myers

Majeux Press
SHERMAN, TEXAS

How Christians Behave
The Foundation Series, Volume Two

© Copyright 2009 by Kenneth N. Myers

Unless otherwise indicated, Scripture is taken from the
HOLY BIBLE, NEW INTERNATIONAL VERSION.
Copyright 1973, 1978, 1984 International Bible Society
Used by permission of Zondervan Bible Publishers.

Myers, Kenneth Neal, 1959-
What Christians Believe/Kenneth N. Myers

ISBN 1-4392-4921-0
LCCN 2009906935

1. Ten Commandments 2. Theology 3. Christian Ethics

238

Cover design: Neal Mayeux
Photograph: *El Mesquita, Cordoba Spain* by Neal Mayeux

Published by Mayeux Press
P.O. Box 3497, Sherman, TX 75091

To
Bishop Ray R. Sutton
who changed my life with his book on covenant.

Acknowledgements

Thank you to the people of Living Word Chapel, Forest, Wisconsin, who in 1986 were the first to explore the Ten Commandments with me.

Thank you to the people of Christ Church Cathedral, Sherman, Texas, whom I have served and loved for seventeen years, and who have also explored these Commandments with me.

Thank you to Scott Rudy and Kenneth Myers II for their editing, proofreading, and suggestions.

Thank you to my wife Shirley whose life exemplifies a woman of the Word.

Table of Contents

Preface to the Series

Too many Christians don't know what it really means to be Christian. Some think that "being good" is what it is all about. Some think that holding a general idea about Jesus - that he died for our sins and rose again from the dead - encompasses all that is needed. Too many, in the modern culture, choose to define for themselves the core definitions of the faith: "well, *for me* being a Christian means..." Others say, "Oh, it's all such a bother. I'll just let the clergy worry about that, and I'll go to church and worship God and live my life."

I would suggest (mimicking here the ancient teachings of the Church) that there are four basic considerations Christians need in order to be fully rounded and secure in their faith.

Belief

What you believe matters. As others have pointed out before me, if you believe five and five makes ten, and you make a five dollar purchase and give the cashier a ten dollar bill, you will not be satisfied with two dollars in change. Belief matters in the real world. It defines us, and it defines our relationships with others - including our relationship with God. Obviously, belief is not just a religious or spiritual matter. Belief affects every aspect of life. If you believe too much sun can cause skin cancer, you will stay out of too much sun. If you believe all Cretans are liars, you won't trust what a Cretan says to you. In the same way, what you believe about God, Jesus, the Church, salvation, and the afterlife has an impact on your every day living, and on your expectations of the future.

Actions

Actions speak louder that words. Everyone has heard this axiom. The Christian faith is not simply a set of theological statements, it also entails how we *act* in our lives. Certainly this flows from our beliefs - real beliefs are played out in what we *do*. Too often people who consider themselves

Christian do none of the things that follow true belief.

Saint James wrote, "Show me your faith without deeds, and I will show you my faith by what I *do*...You see that a person is justified by what he *does* and not by faith alone" (James 2.18,24). Just because you say it doesn't necessarily make it so. Actions matter.

Spirituality

Some people hear the word "spirituality" and think of some kind of mystical spookiness, some kind of otherworldiness that causes super-holy others to walk around as if on a cloud. But *everyone* possesses some form of spirituality. By spirituality, I mean how we relate to God in a genuine personal relationship, and how it impacts our relationship with ourselves and with others. The chief means of cultivating a Christian spirituality is through prayer, and yet many believers either do not pray at all, or else pray very haltingly, not really knowing *how* to pray.

When we read about godly men and women of the past, we realize they were all people of prayer, including Jesus who, though he was God come in the flesh, made it his habit to spend quality time in prayer, and to teach others how to do the same.

Worship

Finally, Christians who are well-rounded in their faith are people who worship God, and they worship God together with other believers. Far from being a coincidental aspect of true faith, worshipping God with the Church is core to what it means to be Christian. The writer of Hebrews admonished his readers, "Let us not give up meeting together, as some are in the habit of doing, but let us encourage one another - and all the more as you see the Day approaching" (Hebrews 10.25). Just as in the case of prayer, many Christians have no idea *how* to worship. Worship may be seen by some as simply singing a few songs and listening to a sermon. Others insist they don't need to gather with God's people and worship because they can worship God alone out in nature. Still others consider themselves too holy to stoop to gathering with lesser beings and simply stay at home and "do their own thing", while others do nothing at all. None of these folk realize that the Bible has much to say about the "what" and the "how" of worship.

A Fourfold Plan

I propose four volumes outlining the Christian faith in popular, easy to understand fashion.

Volume One deals with what Christians believe, and focuses on the ancient Creeds of the Church which capsulize true belief.

Volume Two deals with how Christians behave, and focuses on the ethics given by God to Moses in the Ten Commandments.

Volume Three deals with how Christians pray, and focuses on the model Jesus gave his disciples in response to their request that he teach them to pray - the Lord's Prayer or the Our Father.

Volume Four deals with how Christians worship, and focuses on the two aspects of biblical worship: Word and Sacraments.

It should be said that these books are written first and primarily from a Christian perspective which believes the Bible to be the authoritative Word of God and believes that God has moved in his Church and directed it throughout history. It is also written from an Anglican perspective, a viewpoint that sees

itself as "Catholic" (that is, rooted in the ancient, undivided faith) and
"Protestant" (that is, calling for a continual reformation of the people of God, having the Holy Scriptures as an unerring guide to all matters of belief, action, spirituality and worship). The Anglican faith in one sense finds its roots all the way back with the Apostles, and in another sense finds its roots in the ancient Celtic/British/English church - the church of St. Patrick, St. Columba, St. Hilda, and more recently, influential Christians like C.S. Lewis, J. I. Packer, and a host of others.

If the words of these books have a decidedly Anglican focus, the things to which they speak are much more broad in scope and possess a truth that can be shared by all Christians. My prayer is that these volumes will be used as instruments to enrich all Christians who study them, whatever their denomination or tradition.

Finally, anyone addressing the topics before us - from what Christians believe to how Christians worship - finds himself confronted with an inexhaustible amount of data. Literally millions of sermons on these subjects have been preached over the course of the last 2000 years. Thousands of books have been written about them. The goal of this series is not to be exhaustive, nor even to say everything that is important about the subjects at hand, but to provide a popular level of understanding, thoroughly rooted in Scripture . These books are intentionally designed to be used in personal reading, Sunday School classes, and small group studies. You will notice that the chapters are chock-full of Scriptures. Please do not give in to the temptation to skip over the Scripture texts, thinking you already know what they say. Let them speak to you in a new and fresh way. While I recognize that I can't say everything worthy of being said, I do truly hope that what is written here will stir up minds and hearts and cause people to dig deeper into other resources. I have appended a suggested reading list at the end. What we have before us when we deal with these noble subjects is treasure. It is worth digging for.

Introduction

The DNA Of The Bible

Before we talk about the Ten Commandments, let's talk for a minute about movies and good stories. I'm going to share with you two quick ones.

The first is set in a dusty Old West town somewhere out in the rough mountains of Texas. The small village is beset by a tough gang of outlaws who have taken control of the place. The people of the town are having their lives ruined by the bad guys. The gang rides into town, causing havoc, shooting up the place, leaving dead bodies in the street, disrupting the peaceful life of the good citizens. Unexpectedly, a hero appears, but he doesn't look like a hero. He has weaknesses, is kind hearted, and seems puny. But he shows bravery and takes on the bad guys. At first it looks like he's going to lose, but the tables turn and he cleans up the town and restores peace. Of course, the prettiest maiden in the village falls in love with him and they get married and have children and live together happily ever after.

The next story is set in some far-flung galaxy in an imaginary science fiction time of "a long, long time ago". The planet of peace-loving people find themselves taken over by an evil intergalactic force which disrupts their lives and runs roughshod over them. Unexpectedly, an unlikely young hero with a light saber and a fast space ship shows up. At first everyone agrees he is a nobody - a nothing - but then they see he is really the champion. He fights against the evil empire, almost loses his life, but in the end destroys their gigantic starship and liberates the people. And there is a love story here, too.

Did you notice the similarities? The only basic difference is between six-shooters and laser swords, fast horses and flying machines. The fact that the stories are basically the same is not an accident. It is called a *meta-story* - the same basic tale, told in a different setting. Most good stories share a kind of common DNA.

Speaking of DNA, did you know that the code for your entire bodily make-up is contained in every single cell of your body? I am no expert on DNA, but here is what I know: the basic data of your body is contained, like a little computer program, in every fiber of your being. Scientists can take a cell from anywhere in your body and find all the information they need about who you are: your skin color, your hair and eye color, your basic propensity for diseases and weaknesses, your family relations, and everything else about you.

The DNA Of The Bible

Just like the good stories having a *meta-story*, and just like your body having DNA in every cell, the Bible has a kind of DNA that is woven throughout the whole thing. Once you see it, you see it everywhere. It is called the *covenant model*[1], and whereas your body's DNA has a long and complicated string to it, the Bible's DNA has only five points. I am convinced that if you were to make an effort to

---

[1] What follows may be found in detail in Ray Sutton's *That You May Prosper*, Dominion Press, Fort Worth, TX, 1987. I count this as one of the five books that have changed my life, and I highly recommend it to you.

memorize the five points of covenant, you would suddenly find yourself making a lot more sense of the Bible, from Genesis all the way through to Revelation (more about that later).

To set the stage for the five points of covenant, let me share one more story. A great and powerful king of a world empire - let's say the king of ancient Babylon, or Persia, or Rome - arrives to rescue a small nation from the hand of some evil despot. After freeing the people from the oppressor, he offers to make covenant with them. It doesn't matter where you turn in ancient literature, the covenant model was always the same. First the king establishes that he is the one in charge (there is no bargaining here; it is a take it or leave it deal). Secondly, he names and puts in place the leadership which will represent him. Third, he lays out clearly and in writing what is expected of the people. Fourth, he details what will happen if the people keep their end of the deal, and what will happen if they don't. Fifth and finally, the king makes it clear how the covenant continues into the future - how new generations reaffirm the covenant, how new leadership is installed. Simple enough? OK, now let's dig in.

Transcendence

The first point of covenant is called *transcendence*. In this section of the covenant, the king firmly establishes that he is the one in charge. He is transcendent - above and beyond - the situation. In a very real sense, he isn't a player in the game, he is over and above the game. He determines the rules. The question asked in this first point is, "Who makes the rules?" And the answer is, "The king makes the rules. The transcendent one calls the shots."

Hierarchy

The second point of covenant is called *hierarchy*. The great king has no intention of hanging around in the smaller country for the rest of his life. He is going back to his palace, hanging gardens, and servants. But, he is going to leave someone there to officially represent him - someone to speak on his behalf. It may be his son, the prince, or it may be an appointed governor, but whoever it is, this person (or these persons) carries the very authority of the king with them. They can't make the rules (only the king can do that), but they can see to it that the king's rules are followed. The question asked in this second point of covenant is, "Who enforces the rules?" And the answer is, "The king's appointed hierarchy enforces the rules set by the king".

Ethics

The third point of covenant is called *ethics*. In this section of the written, signed, and sealed covenant, the king clearly states what is expected of the people in order for them to keep this covenantal arrangement with the king. This is the section where all the rules are clearly spelled out. These rules are not subject to debate, nor are they arrived at by some kind of democratic process or some bargaining deal-making. The king simply says, "I am the one in charge, and if you are going to walk in covenant with me, here is what you have to do." The question asked in this third point of covenant is, "What are the rules?" And the answer is, "The rules are whatever the king says they are."

Sanctions

The fourth point of covenant is called *sanctions*. In the covenant document, all the consequences of keeping the rules or breaking the rules are spelled out clearly. There can be no real covenant without consequences. The biblical language of sanctions is "blessings and curses". The blessings and the curses come, not arbitrarily, but as the consequences of the people honoring the covenant made. If the people keep the covenant, "all these blessings" come upon them. If they break the covenant, "all these curses" come upon them. The question asked in this fourth point of covenant is, "What are the consequences of keeping or breaking the rules?" And the answer is, "The consequences of keeping the covenant are these blessings, and the consequences of breaking the covenant are these curses".

Continuity

The fifth point of covenant is called *continuity*. The final thing all these ancient covenants establish is how the covenant continues into the future. Sooner or later the king is going to die, so when his son, the prince, becomes the king, how is the covenant renewed? Or, when the children of the original covenant people grow up, how do they renew the covenant with the king? This is also called the *succession clause*. The question asked in this fifth point of covenant is, "How does this covenant continue into the future?" And the answer is, "This covenant continues by future generations renewing and keeping the covenant".

Covenant in the Bible

I wish I could take time here to write an entire detailed book on how the Bible is full of this covenant model. But then, that would be a completely different book from this one, and it has already been written anyway, by a far better writer - Bishop Ray Sutton's *That You May Prosper*. So, for the moment, let me show you just a few places where this covenant model comes into play in the Bible.

- It is found in the original mandate given by God to Adam (Genesis 1 & 2).

- It is found as the structure of the Pentateuch, the first five books of the Bible.

- It is, particularly, the structure of the book of Deuteronomy.

- It is the basic model for most, if not all, the books of the prophets, who were themselves covenant representatives reminding Israel that God had established covenant with them and they were breaking it.

• It is the structure of the Gospel of Matthew.

• It is the structure of the book of Romans.

These are only a handful of the places you will find this model in the pages of the Holy Scriptures. Before leaving the subject, I would like to point out two more significant places you will find this model.

Covenant And The Book Of Revelation

The book of Revelation is clearly a covenant document. It is not a book of *revelations* (plural), but a book of *"The revelation of Jesus Christ, which God gave him to show his servants what must soon take place"* (Revelation 1.1). This book has been, especially in our own age, a much misunderstood prophecy, with modern day hucksters trying to interpret it with the Bible in one hand and a newspaper in the other. People have tried to read into it whatever current situation they found themselves in, missing entirely the point made in the first verse - it was given to show what "must soon take place". Soon, in a first century context, not a twenty first century one.

Here is a very brief outline of the book of Revelation:

Transcendence (Chapter 1): In which John has a vision of the transcendent Lord, the "alpha and omega", the "beginning and the end". John sees Jesus as the King of kings who establishes the new *covenant* (and hence a new five points of covenant).

Hierarchy (Chapters 2 and 3): in which letters are written to the *angels* - the *messengers* (Greek: *angelos*)- the bishops - of the emerging new covenant people. In particular, Jesus is speaking to the bishops under the Apostle John's care in Asia Minor.

Ethics (Chapters 4 and 5): in which we see the throne room scene in heaven, where the Lamb of God opens the seven-sealed scroll (a seven-sealed scroll was a covenant document - a will - sealed by seven witnesses). Here is declared the new ethic for the Church. I would also point out that in this scene the Lamb alone is worthy to open this New Covenant and establish it with his people, and what follows is worship and praise around the throne of God with consequent results in the earth below.

Sanctions (chapters 6 through 19): in which we find the negative consequences of breaking the covenant poured out upon unfaithful Israel. The bulk of the book is a detailing of these curses, which mimic the curses poured out upon Egypt in the book of Exodus - now being poured out upon a singularly called out nation which chose to reject the Messiah and instead join league with Caesar - the "Beast" who was soon to destroy the nation.

Continuity (Chapters 20 through 22): in which a new covenant people emerge from the downfall of ancient Judaism - the "bride of Christ", the "heavenly Jerusalem", the Church of Jesus (cf. Hebrews 12.22-24).

The book of Revelation is not, primarily, about our future. It is about the future of the generation that saw Jesus in the flesh. It was written to encourage the struggling, newly emerging Church to endure to the end and to have hope that victory was theirs. While there is application for our lives and our future (just as with any other book of the Bible), it was written to show "what must soon take place". This book is not a crystal ball through which we gaze in search of nuclear holocausts and an emerging evil world leader. It is a covenant document, spelling out the demise of the Old Covenant - "By calling this covenant 'new', he has made the first one obsolete; and what is obsolete and aging will soon disappear" (Hebrews 8.13) - and the establishing of the New Covenant made with us by our Lord Jesus Christ.

The Covenant And The Commandments

Now that you have something of a feel for the covenant model, and see how it permeates the whole of the Bible, let's turn our attention to the Ten Commandments. If you haven't guessed it by now, the Ten Commandments are thoroughly soaked in the covenant structure.

These commandments are actually called "The Ten Words" (also called the *decalogue*, which means *ten words*) and they are the covenant mandate, the ethics, given by God, through Moses, to the people he had rescued from bondage and was bringing into the freedom of the Promised Land. Exodus 20, in which we find the Ten Commandments, begins, "And God spoke all these words". The transcendent Lord (Yahweh) is giving the stipulations for the covenant.

God has just delivered Israel from the tyrant's hand and brought them out of Egypt.

He has cared for them on their journey, leading them with his very presence, and feeding them with food from heaven. He has initiated covenant with them, that he will be their God and they will be his people, and now he calls his covenant representative, his hierarchy, Moses, up to Mount Sinai to give him the ethics of the covenant. These are the rules by which the people of Israel will keep covenant with their God and deliverer.

Just to make it clear that this is a covenant document, I should point out a couple more often overlooked facts.

In ancient times when a covenant was drawn up, there were two copies made - one for each party. The documents were kept in safekeeping in a kind of "safety-deposit box" in the temple of whatever god the parties worshipped. So it is here. God gave Moses two copies. When we think of Moses coming down from Mount Sinai holding two tablets in his hands, we tend to think of the first tablet having five commandments and the second tablet having the next five. The truth is, Moses came down with two copies[2] (Deuteronomy 10.5). One was his copy - to be safely deposited in the Tabernacle, the house of his

---

[2] cf. Sutton, p. 215.

God; the other was God's copy - also to be safely deposited in God's own house!

These two copies of the *ethics* of the covenant between God and Israel were to be held in a special box called the Ark of the *Covenant*. Also kept in the Ark was Aaron's rod (a symbol of legitimate *hierarchy*) and a pot of manna (a symbol of *sanctions* - blessings - given by God). The Ark was not to be touched by human hands (it represented *transcendence*), and it was to be carried everywhere Israel went on her sojourn (*continuity*). Truly, you see, it was a chest of covenant!

The Ten Commandments are recorded in several places in the Bible, most notably in Exodus 20.1-17:

> And God spoke all these words:
>
> "I am the Lord your God, who brought you out of Egypt, out of the land of slavery.
>
> "You shall have no other gods before me.
>
> "You shall not make for yourself an idol in the form of anything in heaven above or on the earth

beneath or in the waters below. You shall not bow down to them or worship them; for I, the Lord your God, am a jealous God, punishing the children for the sin of the fathers to the third and fourth generation of those who hate me, but showing love to a thousand [generations] of those who love me and keep my commandments.

"You shall not misuse the name of the Lord your God, for the Lord will not hold anyone guiltless who misuses his name.

"Remember the Sabbath day by keeping it holy. Six days you shall labor and do all your work, but the seventh day is a Sabbath to the Lord your God. On it you shall not do any work, neither you, nor your son or daughter, nor your manservant or maidservant, nor your animals, nor the alien within your gates. For in six days the Lord made the heavens and the earth, the sea, and all that is in them, but he rested on the seventh day. Therefore the Lord blessed the Sabbath day and made it holy.

"Honor your father and your mother, so that you may live long in the land the Lord your God is giving you.

"You shall not murder.

"You shall not commit adultery.

"You shall not steal.

"You shall not give false testimony against your neighbor.

"You shall not covet your neighbor's house. You shall not covet your neighbor's wife, or his manservant or maidservant, his ox or donkey, or anything that belongs to your neighbor."

There are ten commandments, and they are simply the covenant model twice told. The first five line out the five points of covenant, and then so do the next five. We will explore this further in each chapter of this book, but as a handy reference here is a chart to follow.

Covenant	First Five	Second Five
Transcendence	You Shall Have No Other Gods Before God	You Shall Not Kill
Hierarchy	You Shall Not Bow Down To Idols	You Shall Not Commit Adultery
Ethics	You Shall Not Misuse God's Name	You Shall Not Steal
Sanctions	Remember The Sabbath	You Shall Not Bear False Witness
Continuity	Honor Your Father And Your Mother	You Shall Not Covet

In the pages that follow, we will visit each of these covenant stipulations and discover how they guide us in our lives. God gave them to his people, not as tools of oppression, but as weapons to guard our freedom. He has delivered us from evil. He has set us free from bondage, and in these ten simple words he gives us the means of living in joy, freedom and victory.

Prologue

The Purpose Of The Law

Christians are totally confused about the Law. On the one hand, they recognize that God gave it to Israel, and that it truly reflects his own character. On the other hand, they have heard and believed (and are correct) that the Law condemns mankind because none of us can keep it, and that Christians are not under the Law. No one can stand before God and say, "Lord, I come before you on the basis of having kept your Word completely and I have never once broken it." Obviously, the lynchpin of the Gospel is that we are all sinners, saved from the curse of the Law by the sacrifice of Jesus Christ on the Cross.

So, what do we do with the Law, with the Ten Commandments? There are two

extremes. Some radicals have simply thrown
them out - "There are no ethics to live by as
Christians, just faith in Jesus. All is fair now.
You can live as you please and that's just
peachy with God. Since all your sins have
been paid for on the cross, then it doesn't
matter what you do". Others, on the opposite
side, have said, "Yes, Christ saved you, but if
you don't keep the rules you have rejected his
salvation, and consequently you are going to
burn in hell." You have probably heard both
these lines of argument, and you have
probably also come to the conclusion that both
of these miss the mark of the balance that the
Bible teaches. So, what *does* the Bible, and
specifically the New Testament (the New
Covenant), say about the Law?

The Law Is Good Stuff

Do you find it interesting that the Old
Testament is considered part of the canon of
Holy Scriptures for Christians? If the radicals
were correct, we would just toss out the whole
Old Testament, and, in fact, this is what some
early Church heretics attempted to do.
Marcion, the first great heretic (ca. 85-160)
went so far as to declare the Old Testament to
be the record of a completely different god -
that Yahweh was *not* the Father of Jesus
Christ! Marcion threw out the Old Testament,

but in order to do that, he had to throw out about half the New Testament too - he ripped out three of the four Gospels, the epistles of James and John and Jude, the book of Hebrews, and some of Paul's writings. All he was left with was a handful of carefully edited epistles of Paul and the Gospel of John. And there is the problem. You can't have the New Covenant in whole without the Old Covenant too. The New Testament is saturated with the Old. It is built upon the Old, and to destroy the old writings is to destroy the foundation of the new writings.

Contrary to Marcion, Jesus confirmed that the Law was good stuff: "Do not think that I have come to abolish the Law or the Prophets; I have not come to abolish them but to fulfill them...Anyone who breaks one of the least of these commandments and teaches others to do the same will be called least in the kingdom of heaven, but whoever *practices* and *teaches* these commands will be called great in the kingdom of heaven" (Matthew 5.17-19).

When people look for an excuse to eliminate a good helping of the Law from their spiritual diets, they often turn to Saint Paul, the Apostle of Grace, who spent so much of his writing showing that Christians are free from the curse of the Law. But Paul himself shows that the Law is not in opposition to a life of faith, but is actually at one with such a life. "Do we then nullify the law by this faith? Not at all! Rather, we uphold the law" (Romans 3.31). The problem is not with the Law, Paul points out, but with us. The Law is a pure reflection of the heart of God, but we fallen and sinful humans are incapable of keeping it. He wrote, "So then, the law is holy, and the commandment is holy, righteous and good" (Romans 7.12).

The problem Paul (and Jesus, and all the Apostles) had with the Law was not the Commandments themselves, but the *misuse* of the commandments. The New Covenant doesn't stand over against the Old Covenant, it stands over against the abuse of the Old Covenant, which was rampant in the days of Jesus and the Apostles. When Paul wrote to his protege, the young Bishop Timothy of Ephesus, he said, "We know that the law is good, if one *uses it properly*" (1 Timothy 1.8). What, then, is the proper use of the law?

The Law Can't Save Us

Some people have made an erroneous distinction between the Old and New Testaments. They have suggested that in the Old Testament era, God dealt with his people in one way - through the keeping of the Law, and that in the New Testament era, God deals with his people in another way - through grace. But the Old Testament is full of stories of the people of God breaking the Ten Commandments. Some of our biblical heroes, like Moses and Gideon and David, broke one or more of the Commandments but were still "saved" - they were still God's chosen and they lived in his blessings and died in his favor. The Law was never a means of salvation. This is of supreme importance to understand. Let it sink in: *the Law was never a means of salvation.*

The reason that keeping the Law was not, is not, and cannot be a means of salvation is that no one can keep it. Saint Paul told the Christians in Rome, "Therefore no one will be declared righteous by observing the law, rather, through the law we become conscious of sin" (Romans 3.20). And to the Galatian Christians he wrote, "Know that a man is not justified by observing the law, but by faith in Jesus Christ" (Galatians 2.16). Just to make sure they understood it, he said it again: "Clearly no one is justified before God by the law, because 'The righteous will live by faith'" (Galatians 3.11).

"No one" includes everyone. You can't name a single person, from Adam to the last man on earth, who is justified because he kept the law perfectly. The only person that has kept the law in whole is Jesus himself, "who has been tempted in every way, just as we are - yet was without sin" (Hebrews 4.15). Name a great Old Testament man or woman of God - Abraham, Sarah, Moses, David, Hannah, Deborah, Isaiah, Jeremiah - all of them were law-breakers; none of them were able to keep wholly the beautiful rules of life given by God which reflected his character.

No, the only way that *anyone* - from Adam to the last - is saved, is through the grace of God: "For it is by grace you have been saved, through faith - and this not from yourselves, it is the gift of God - not by works, so that no one can boast" (Ephesians 2.8-9). God did not deal with Old Testament believers on a different basis than he deals with New Testament believers. When Paul, the New Testament author, says "The righteous will live by faith", he was quoting an Old Testament prophet (Habbakuk 2.4). And the father of all who live by faith was also the father of the Old Testament people of God, Abraham, who "believed [had faith in] God, and it was *credited* to him as righteousness (Galatians 3.6, cf. Genesis 15.6).

The Purpose Of The Law

The Law was never intended by God as a means of salvation. It was never given as the basis of eternal life. What, then, is the purpose of the Law?

First, the Law is given to show us that we need help. Since it is indeed a reflection of God's very character, and it is the ethics of God's covenant with us, the fact that we can't keep it completely and without fail is an indication to us that we are really messed up and we need rescue. In this, the Law serves as something that *points us to Jesus*. If we have all broken the Law (and we have), then none of us has the ground to stand on to come before God based on our own goodness, our own righteousness. We all must approach the throne of the Great King (remember *transcendence*?), recognizing that we enter his presence based upon some other condition than our own deserving. In the book of Galatians, one of Saint Paul's two masterful treatises on Law and Grace (along with Romans), the Apostle uses the analogy of a schoolmaster who is responsible for training a child until he is mature enough to be passed on to a better instructor. "So the law was put in charge," Paul tells us, "to lead us to Christ, that we might be justified by faith" (Galatians

3.24). Before Christ, "the whole world [was] a prisoner of sin" (Galatians 3.22) - the whole world had failed at passing the test that the schoolmaster handed out. But the whole point of the test was to show us we couldn't pass it in our own strength. We needed someone to free us from the condemnation of failing - and that someone was Jesus Christ, who kept the Law completely, yet died, *on our behalf,* the death of a sinner. It is through him that we are reconciled, through him that we are saved, through him that we are made right with God. The Law does its work when it convinces us that we need the grace of God.

But there is a second purpose of the Law. When Paul writes that the Law is good, "if one uses it properly" (1 Timothy 1.8), we must ask the question, "What is the proper use of the Law?"

What I am about to share with you is not simply a New Testament spin on an Old Testament truth. What you are about to see is that, even in the Old Testament, there was a "proper use" of the Law. Please pay careful attention to this next bit.

The principle of *cause and effect* is true in all of life. Anything we do serves as a *cause* that brings about a desired (or undesired) *effect.* This is no less true in the arena of moral matters. A child's disobedience causes the effect of discipline. An adult's breaking of civil law causes the effect of a fine or imprisonment. Now, here is the question: If obedience to the Commandments is the cause, then what is the effect? Legalists (both Jewish and Christian) might tell you the effect is salvation. But we have already seen, in both the Old and New Testaments, that the Law doesn't save us. Think about it! We have all broken the Law, and our subsequent attempts at keeping it cannot effect the forgiveness of sins already committed. The Law is like a precious vase worth thousands of dollars. If you chip the vase in just one place, you have chipped the whole vase. "For whoever keeps the whole law and yet stumbles at just one point is guilty of breaking all of it" (James 2.10). No, if keeping the Law is the *cause*, the *effect* is not salvation or forgiveness or right standing with God.

What then? If we do not keep the Law as a means of gaining God's acceptance, why keep it at all? Watch the common thread in the following Old Testament passages (I will help you out by highlighting the important words).

• Walk in all the way that the Lord your God has commanded you, so that you may *live* and *prosper* and prolong your days in the land that you will possess (Deuteronomy 5.22).

• Carefully follow the terms of this covenant, so that you may *prosper* in everything you do (Deuteronomy 29.9).

• Do not let this Book of the Law depart from your mouth; meditate on it day and night, so that you may be careful to do everything written in it. Then you will be *prosperous* and *successful* (Joshua 1.8).

• In everything that he undertook in the service of God's temple and in obedience to the law and the commands, he sought his God and worked wholeheartedly. And so he *prospered* (2 Chronicles 31.21).

• Blessed is the man who does not walk in the counsel of the wicked or stand in the way of sinners or sit in the seat of mockers. But his delight is in the law of the Lord, and on his law he meditates day and night. He is like a tree planted by streams of water, which yields its fruit in season and whose leaf does not wither. *Whatever he does prospers* (Psalm 1.1-3).

Now, let me ask the question again. Why follow the Law? *Because it brings prosperity and dominion*! The cause is obedience to God's Word. The effect is prosperity and dominion in this life and the next. Show me a people, a civilization, a culture, a family, a church, that lives by the Word of God and I will show you a people who ultimately prosper and win. Show me a people who live by their own selfish rules and I will show you a people who are quickly doomed to poverty and destruction.

One caveat: we should not be so foolish as to understand this in some magical sense, thinking that we can obey God's Word and so manipulate him into giving us what we want. Neither should we understand this as some kind of fast-track, "name it and claim it" prosperity mechanism. Prosperity and victory occur over time, as God's people are ethically faithful to the covenant. One generation's faithfulness may not bring automatic prosperity and victory, but it will prepare a foundation for following generations, ultimately bringing God's blessings in full. King David cautions us to "not fret" because of the prosperity of evil men, for "in a little while...the wicked will be no more...but the meek will inherit the land and enjoy great peace" (Psalm 37.1-11). It is the *long haul* that we must think about. Living our lives according to God's Word, and teaching future generations to do the same, will lead to inevitable prosperity and victory. "Time", as the song says, "is on my side" - on *our* side.

Of course, this doesn't mean that all the blessings of God are waiting for the future. It doesn't mean that we sow all the seeds of obedience and only our children get to reap them. We do indeed enjoy the benefits of the Kingdom of God as we faithfully keep his Word. But what we experience is only a foretaste of the covenantal blessings laid up for those who will follow after us if we are faithful to instill the covenant into them (hence, *continuity*).

Truly Keeping the Commandments

I know a fellow who, when he gets into a tight spot, wants to keep the Commandments so he will get the blessings. It doesn't work that way. The mere outward observance of the Commandments is a false observance. True obedience consists of three things[3].

Motivation: Unless obedience is motivated by a heart attitude, it is not true obedience. The first commandment is that we

---

[3] cf. Sutton, p. 62ff.

have no other gods than God himself. To genuinely keep the commandments of God we must keep them with integrity of heart, thought and action. When Jesus was asked what was the greatest of all the commandments, he quoted Deuteronomy 6.4-6: "Hear, O Israel: The Lord our God, the Lord is one. Love the Lord your God with all your heart and with all your soul and with all your strength. These commandments that I give you today are to be *upon your hearts*" (cf. Matthew 22.37-40).

Standards: If we are to be obedient, there must be something to obey. The verse quoted above says, "these *commandments* that I give you..." God has given us absolute standards which we are to obey. To say we know God, and yet do not obey him, is a lie. Saint John wrote, "The man who says, 'I know him,' but does not do what he commands is a liar, and the truth is not in him" (1 John 2.4).

Application: The standards of God, obeyed out of a heart motivated by faith in God, must be applied to the specific situations of our lives. Oftentimes we must follow the spirit of the Law rather than the letter. Saint Paul makes this clear: "He has made us competent as ministers of a new covenant - not of the letter but of the Spirit; for the letter kills, but the Spirit gives life" (2 Corinthians 3.6). An example of this is found in the prostitute Rahab, who lied to protect the Hebrew spies from certain death. By this seeming act of breaking the Law, she was brought into a covenant relationship with God and his people (Joshua 2; 6.22-25). The truth of the matter is, she acted out of a heart motivated by faith, applying the law of the Spirit. Later it is said of her, "By faith the prostitute Rahab, because she welcomed the spies, was not killed with those who were disobedient" (Hebrews 11.31). Rahab would later figure into the genealogy of King David, and of David's greater son, Jesus Christ. This is not the same as situation ethics, where any given situation determines what is right and wrong. Here, the standard is a standard set by God by which all things must be measured.

Live Long And Prosper

If you are a fan of *Star Trek* (and who isn't?), you will remember the Vulcan greeting and blessing that Mr. Spock often made. Holding his hand up with fingers split into a V-shape, he would say, "Live long and prosper". What many do not know is that Mr. Spock, the actor Leonard Nimoy, borrowed this from his childhood days in the Orthodox

Jewish synagogue, where the rabbi would lift his hands and make the Hebrew letter *shin*, the first letter of *Shaddai* (meaning "Almighty"), and speak a blessing over the people.

When Leonard Nimoy was creating the Mr. Spock character for "Star Trek" in 1966, he remembered a thrilling moment from his childhood Orthodox synagogue. It was Yom Kippur, and the Kohanim, representatives of the priestly tribe, swayed on the bimah, their long tallitot draped over their heads, their fingers spread in a V-shape.

"These men didn't say the blessing, they shouted it," Nimoy said in his resonant, gravelly voice. "They chanted and wailed, and everyone had their eyes covered, and my father said to me, 'Don't Look!' And of course, being 8 years old, I peeked, and I saw them doing this with their hands, and it was very chilling, passionate, ecstatic, fervent, theatrical."[4]

The full Aaronic blessing, spoken to this day in synagogues and churches around the world, is found in Numbers 6.23-27: "Tell Aaron and his sons, 'This is how you are to bless the Israelites. Say to them: "The Lord bless you and keep you; the Lord make his face shine upon you and be gracious to you; the Lord turn his face toward you and give you peace."' So they will put my name on the Israelites, and I will bless them."

Nimoy, a faithful Jew to this day, knew well how to summarize the blessing in just a few words: "Live long and prosper". And *this* is the purpose of the Law - that in keeping it you might be blessed; that you will, "*live* and *prosper* and *prolong your days* in the land that you will possess" (Deuteronomy 5.33).

---

[4] *Bimah Me Up, Scotty,* by Naomi Pfefferman, JewishJournal.com, December 4, 2003.

Chapter One

No Other Gods

*""I am the Lord your God, who brought you out of
Egypt, out of the land of slavery. You shall have no
other gods before me."*

God is in charge. God is the only one in
charge. The first point of covenant is
transcendence, and it asks the question "Who
makes the rules?" In the first commandment,
God establishes the fact that he is the one in
command.

"Well, why should *you* be in charge?"
some other god might ask (or some other
religious leader who *thinks* he represents some

other god). The Jewish rabbis had an answer for this. They point out that the Commandments were not given *at the beginning* of the story of Israel's redemption, but *after* he had performed wonderful acts on their behalf. It is not as if God just rode into town and named himself the new sheriff! He begins the covenant stipulations by saying, "I am the Lord your God, who brought you out of Egypt, out of the land of slavery."

The Basis For God's Claim

Laying aside for a moment that God is the Creator and sustainer of life, and that it was he who brought Israel into existence in the first place, God begins this covenant by reminding the Jews that he is the one who set them free from bondage. For more than four hundred years they had been strangers in a strange land, dwelling under the oppression of a foreign king who worshipped foreign gods (including himself as an incarnation of a god). But through the mighty acts of the Exodus, God brought plagues on Egypt, protected Israel, led them through parted waters at the Red Sea, and supplied them with food for their journey toward the land he had promised their forefathers. His basis for demanding their loyalty - if they were willing to make covenant with him - was *deliverance*. They were once in bondage, and now they were free, because of his mighty acts.

In the New Testament, this theme would be picked up again by Jesus and the Apostles, who showed that the deliverance begun in the Exodus continued in the death and resurrection of Jesus, by which we have been delivered from the bondage of sin. Interestingly, when Moses and Elijah appeared on the Mount of Transfiguration and talked to Jesus (talk about the communion of saints!), the Bible tells us that they spoke with him, "about his *departure*" - literally, in Greek, "about his *exodus*". J.I. Packer writes, "The God who redeemed Jews from Egyptian slavery has redeemed Christians from bondage to sin and to Satan at the cost of Calvary. Now it is by keeping his law that the liberty thus secured is to be preserved"[5]. To not keep his law is to slide right back into the bondage from which we have been freed.

This same God who delivered Israel is the God who delivers us in Christ Jesus. Such a statement may be taken for granted by Christians today, but there is a very important truth behind it: God is One. The greatest

---

[5] Packer, J.I., *Keeping the 10 Commandments*, Crossway Books, Wheaton, Ill, 2007, p. 43.

commandment in the Old Testament, according to Jesus, begins, "Hear, O Israel: the Lord our God, the Lord is one" (Deuteronomy 6.4). Jesus is not *another* God, a second God in a corporate deity of three. There is only one God, and he has come to us in the flesh in the person of Jesus Christ. The very idea of transcendence demands singularity. If there were two, or three, or ten thousand of something, then that something would not be "totally other", "unique", or to use a biblical word, "holy". The early Church father Justin Martyr (a Samaritan who died a martyr in Rome in 165) wrote to the Jewish philosopher Trypho, "There will never be another God, Trypho, and there has been no other since the world began...than he who made and ordered the universe. We do not think that our God is different from yours. He is the same who brought your fathers out of Egypt 'by his powerful hand and his outstretched arm.' We do not place our hope in some other god, for there is none, but in the same God as you do: the God of Abraham, Isaac and Jacob".[6]

God, the transcendent One, declares that he alone is to be worshipped and served. As with the rest of the first five

----

[6] Justin Martyr, *Dialogue with Trypho the Jew*, 11.1.

commandments, this one is divided into two parts: the command, and the reason for the command. Here, the reason is given first: he has delivered us out Egypt (sin, the world). He is our God not only by reason of *creation*, but even more significantly, by reason of *redemption*. Saint Paul says it another way: "He has rescued us from the dominion of darkness and brought us into the kingdom of the Son he loves, in whom we have redemption, the forgiveness of sins" (Colossians 1.13-14).

Worshipping Other Gods

In all times and places people worship "other gods" in the form of false religions and manmade idols. There are about a dozen primary religions in the world. Some of them are monotheistic, worshipping, as best they understand, the One God. Others have a plethora of gods to whom they pray and worship. All of them possess some of the truth, but Christianity makes the bold claim that it alone possesses the fullness of God's revealed truth, and in particular, the fullness of his revelation in the person of Jesus Christ.

When my son Ken was a teenager there was a popular Christian song that proclaimed, "There's no God like Jehovah!" One day as we were talking, he said to me, "Dad, there's no god like Ganesh, either." Thinking for a split second that my son had lost his mind, I asked him to explain. "Well," he said, "there's no other god with the body of a little boy and the head of an elephant!" I laughed, and readily agreed that he was right. The list of false gods is endless: Ganesh, Ishtar, Diana, Thor, Jupiter, Zeus, Reverend Moon, and countless more. To put these, or any other, in the place of God is to break the first commandment.

But chances are, these are not the temptations we face. I have personally never met a Bible-believing Christian tempted to bow down and worship Thor and his hammer. But I have known Christians who were tempted to substitute a god of their own making for the One, True and Living God. The majority of other gods in our culture are more subtle than Ganesh. I'm going to list nine gods that vie for the place of worship, and to help you remember them, I'm going to conveniently give them all names that begin with *P*. Here then is the *Pantheon of the P Gods*.

Possessions

Western civilization is materialistic. Our success is measured by what we have. We have a tendency to possess things we don't even want in order to "keep up with the Joneses". For many in our culture, including Christians, the acquisition of possessions becomes the chief object of worship, and all their time, thought, and energy is devoted to "getting more".

Plenty

Plenty is the twin brother to the god Possessions. It is the lust for having great wealth, even to the point of securing one's own plenty at the expense of another's bare minimum. The prophets of the Old Testament prophesied against men who "weighted the scales" in order to cheat others and make themselves richer. They may not have a little wooden statue that they pray to, but they are doing what amounts to the same: "Put to death...evil desires and greed, *which is idolatry*" (Colossians 3.5).

Pride

Many Christians break this first commandment by worshipping the god called Pride. The Apostle John tells us that pride is the result of loving the world, and that whoever loves the world, the love of the Father is not in him:

Do not love the world or anything in the world. If anyone loves the world, the love of the Father is not in him: For everything in the world - the cravings of sinful man, the lust of his eyes and *the boasting of what he has and does* - comes not from the Father but from the world. The world and its desires pass away, but the man who does the will of God lives forever (1 John 2.15-17).

This god called Pride is a hard taskmaster, ruining good people and leading them down a path of destruction. "Pride goes before destruction, a haughty spirit before a fall" (Proverbs 16.18).

Power

There is, perhaps, no stronger god in the pantheon of modern deities than the god of Power. The religions that are "power religions", including secular humanism which is so prevalent in our culture, are the chief antagonists to true faith in God. Those who worship the god of Power declare that "I can do it on my own". Their goal is not to please God, but to have more and more power in order to manipulate others to fulfill their own selfish and evil desires. This god manifests itself at every level of society, from the greatest of world leaders to the lowly person who has the chance to lord it over just one other human being. It was Edmund Burke who said it so well: "Power corrupts. Absolute power corrupts absolutely."

Popularity

The god of Popularity is especially prominent among young people, but makes its long tentacles felt among all. To be popular among peers is one of the greatest hindrances to truly following and serving God. It affects business people, celebrities, housewives, clergy, youth, sports figures, children, and every other group in our culture. It has been the god that has turned many Christians away from the faith and sold them a bill of goods that turned out to be, in the end, empty.

Persons

The god called Persons rears his head when people worship other people. Heroes can take the place of God. For many, it is not a matter of what God's Word says, but what "my hero" says. *This is especially true in political and religious circles.* "My pastor" or "my president" can become awful gods if they are not held in their proper places. Here is where cults become cults. This is not to say that we should have no heroes, but that we should not worship them. We should not give them the *carte blanche* loyalty which is reserved for God alone.

Party

The god of Party demands allegiance to "the group". The Democratic or Republican or Libertarian parties come to mind. So do the parties of Communism and Capitalism. Likewise the parties of Anglican and Pentecostal and Baptist. You get the idea - even a good thing can become an evil god if it demands your allegiance without questioning. The problem with parties - all of them - is that they are filled with fallen human beings. Some institutions that begin well end up with a kind of nebulous "angel" - "the god of the party" - which is always asking more and more of the people and always giving less and less. In the end, some parties demand that you die for them in order to keep them afloat. How many lives have been ruined because of compromise or undue sacrifice "for the sake of the company". This god demands you die for it. Only the true God offered to die for you.

Pleasure

The god of Pleasure is perhaps the most worshipped false god in the world today. In fact, many Christians slip into pleasure worship when they pray for their own desires and comforts to be met, never asking or seeking God's will in the matter. God wants his people to have good and prosperous lives, but not at the expense of bending the knee to the god of Pleasure. It really is a matter of priorities, isn't it? Jesus said, "Do not worry, saying, 'What shall we eat?' or 'What shall we drink?' or 'What shall we wear?' For the pagans run after all these things, and your heavenly Father knows that you need them. But seek first his kingdom and his righteousness, and all these things will be given to you as well" (Matthew 6.31-33). Paul warned Timothy that in the last days (in his *own* day, I might add), men will be "lovers of pleasure more than lovers of God" (2 Timothy 3.4). The saying remains true even now. The god of Pleasure is terribly powerful.

Projects

The god of projects draws people's loyalties away from the One True God by busying them with pet concerns. People have left the fellowship of God's family for things like bowling teams, school projects, and other seemingly innocent activities. Harmless enough in themselves - it may even be good and helpful to be part of them - they become false gods when they compromise God's place in our hearts and in our time, demanding what is reserved for him as their own.

There are certainly other gods that could be mentioned here, but the point should be clear by now that even though we may not be seduced by some cultic group or some pagan religious system, the "other gods" of our culture do make demands on our loyalties that must be resisted if we are to remain faithful to Jesus Christ.

Joy Davidman, who would later become the wife of the famous and beloved C.S. Lewis (and whose story is beautifully portrayed in the movie *Shadowlands*), wrote an insightful book on the Ten Commandments in which she described the gods of modern times, but warns that, "we live in an age of lost faith and lost hope and empty hearts. Today the Commandment, 'Thou shalt have no other gods before me,' must include, 'Thou shalt have me.'"[7]

The worship of the One True God demands *total allegiance*. God will not have any half-worship. He will not allow himself to be put up in a pantheon alongside other gods. If we are to be faithful to him, we must love him with *all* our hearts, *all* our souls and *all* our strength.

---

[7] Davidman, Joy, *Smoke On The Mountain*, Westminster Press, Philadelphia, 1954, p. 23.

Chapter Two

You Shall Not Bow Down To Idols

"You shall not make for yourself an idol in the form of anything in heaven above or on the earth beneath or in the waters below. You shall not bow down to them or worship them; for I, the Lord your God, am a jealous God, punishing the children for the sin of the fathers to the third and fourth generation of those who hate me, but showing love to a thousand {generations} of those who love me and keep my commandments."

A little Buddha statue, a funny little Ganesh made from stone, a giant totem pole, some Santeria saint/god in the corner of a Cuban food shop - these are the things we think of when we say the word "idol". But the second commandment is not really about these things. You see, with idols such as these, people worship *other* gods. What this commandment is referring to is some kind of inadequate portrayal of the One True God.

The first commandment tells us to put God first, and it correlates to the first point of covenant, *transcendence*. "You shall have no other gods before me" is spoken in reference to *who* God is; it deals with his *being*. He alone is to be worshipped and served.

The second commandment correlates to the second point of covenant, *hierarchy*, and it is speaks to *how* God's people are to worship *him*. Granted, we shouldn't bow down to the idols of the other gods - that is a given. But as God's called and appointed people, his hierarchy, we shouldn't fashion anything which represents God and worship it. This commandment is about the *proper means of worshipping* the transcendent God.

The Hierarchy At Worship

A serious study of covenant will reveal that there are three covenant institutions created by God, and that each of these three has a hierarchy of leadership. The first is the family (and we will explore this in the fifth commandment), the second is civil government (think Moses, and David, and right down to the civil government under which you live - they are all called to obey the Creator in their governing), and the third is the Church (both the Old and New Testament Church). This commandment addresses how the Church is to worship God.

This is not the place to explore church structures[8], but two things need to be said here. First, there is such a thing as a biblical and historic structure of the Church, with God-ordained leadership at the helm. But the second thing - and what is particularly pertinent to our present subject - is that *all Christians are part of the hierarchy of the Church.* So this commandment isn't just for bishops or pastors or priests or deacons. It is for everyone who comes before God to perform the service of adoration and worship. In the New

---

[8] I refer you to Book One and Four of this series for more discussion of church government.

Testament, the word for priest (Greek *hieros*) is never reserved for a select group within the Church. It is *only* used in the context of all believers. Actually, Saint John is the only one who uses the word, and here is what he says:

> • To him who loves us and has freed us from our sins by his blood, and has made us to be a kingdom and *priests* to serve his God and Father—to him be glory and power for ever and ever! Amen (Revelation 1.6).

> • You have made them to be a kingdom and *priests* to serve our God, and they will reign on the earth (Revelation 5.10).

> • Blessed and holy are those who have part in the first resurrection. The second death has no power over them, but they will be *priests* of God and of Christ and will reign with him for a thousand years (Revelation 20.6).

To which Saint Peter adds,

You also, like living stones, are being built into a spiritual house to be *a holy priesthood*, offering spiritual sacrifices acceptable to God through Jesus Christ...But you are a chosen people, *a royal priesthood*, a holy nation, a people belonging to God, that you may declare the praises of him who called you out of darkness into his wonderful light (1 Peter 2.5, 9).

One of the insights recovered by the Reformers was just this: that all Christians are, by virtue of their baptism, ordained into "the priesthood of all believers". The work of priests is to offer sacrifices to God. In the Christian Church, there is no particular and exclusive group which offers sacrifices. We *all* offer sacrifices, and here are the sacrifices we offer:

> • Therefore, I urge you, brothers, in view of God's mercy, to *offer your bodies as living sacrifices*, holy and pleasing to God - this is your spiritual act of worship (Romans 12.1).

> • I am amply supplied, now that I have received from Epaphroditus the *gifts you sent*. They are a fragrant offering, *an acceptable sacrifice*, pleasing to God (Philippians 4.18).

> • Through Jesus, therefore, let us continually offer to God *a sacrifice of praise*

- the fruit of lips that confess his name. And do not forget to do good and to share with others, for with such *sacrifices* God is pleased (Hebrews 13.15-16).

• You also, like living stones, are being built into a spiritual house to be a holy priesthood, offering *spiritual sacrifices* acceptable to God through Jesus Christ (1 Peter 2.5).

There are, then, four sacrifices which we offer to God: our very selves, our money and possessions, our good deeds, and our praise. These are what Peter calls "spiritual sacrifices".

As with the first commandment, the second is structured with two parts: the command, and the reason for the command. The command is, "don't bow down to idols"; the reason is, "because God is a jealous God, and there will be consequences on you and your children who follow in your ways."

The Enticing Thing About Idols

Ironically, when Moses came down from the mountain carrying the two copies of the Ten Commandments, the first thing he saw was the people breaking about half of them!

There they were, led by Aaron, his brother, engaged in a sexual orgy and dancing around a golden calf that Aaron had crafted from their jewelry (Exodus 32). Interestingly, the people weren't worshipping some false god in this bizarre moment, they were falsely worshipping the True God. They said to one another, "This is your God, O Israel, who brought you up out of Egypt"[9] (Exodus 32.4).

The enticing thing about idolatry is the power it gives the idol worshipper. God forbids us to worship him through idols because idols are things made with human hands. In effect, the idolaters are saying, "*I* can control (manipulate) God, because *I* have created a means of contacting him." *At its root, idolatry is about us manipulating God rather than serving him*; getting him to do what we want rather than us seeking to do his will. Idol worshippers say, "*I* think this is what God is like - he is strong like a bull (or cunning like a snake, or beautiful like a woman) - *I* have discovered God's personality; this statue depicts what he is really like." But obviously, no statue can fully capture God's qualities and characteristics - any human attempt to portray God is inadequate - so there ends up being a

---

[9] The NIV text says, "These are your gods...", but the NIV textual footnote gives the better translation.

plethora of statues and gods, each attempting to capture an aspect of God's nature. You start with a golden calf, and you end up with something like Hinduism.

In contrast to this, the people of God say, "We have not found God on our own! No, he has revealed himself to us. We know what he is like because *he* has shown us." Joy Davidman writes, "Do not think the idolater too foolish to know that his god is man-made and breakable. He does know it; that is precisely the sort of God he wants - a god he can control."[10]

Now, take a step back and look at this thing. Isn't this the precise manner in which many Christians approach God, even though they have never bowed down to a physical idol? They attempt to manipulate him, they pray, in effect, "not your will but mine be done". They live their lives according to their own desires and self-interests, without truly seeking first the kingdom of God. This, my friends, is idolatry. Saint Paul tells us the same, "Put to death, therefore, whatever belongs to your earthly nature: sexual immorality, impurity, lust, evil desires and greed, *which is idolatry*" (Colossians 3.5).

---

[10] Davidman, p. 33.

The Consequences of Idolatry

Have you ever known a family, religion or culture steeped in idolatry that endured as a successful and prosperous institution for the long haul? Nope. It doesn't happen. Because there are consequences to idolatry. Whether that idol is a statue of stone or simply trying to manipulate God for selfish ends, the idolaters always end up at the bottom of the totem pole. They are not the head, they are the tail. They are not the winners, they are the losers. Their culture becomes one of poverty and oppression. Here is why.

The second commandment continues,

> for I, the Lord your God, am a jealous God, punishing the children for the sin of the fathers to the third and fourth generation of those who hate me, but showing love to a thousand {generations} of those who love me and keep my commandments (Exodus 20.5-6).

"Punishing the children". Some people have read this and thought how unfair of God to punish the children for the sins of their fathers. But this is a misunderstanding of the text and of God's style and method. The Law says, "Fathers shall not be put to death for their children, nor children put to death for their fathers; each is to die for his own sin" (Deuteronomy 24.16). What the second commandment means is something completely different.

The King James Version is a better translation here: "visiting the iniquity of the fathers upon the children unto the third and fourth generation of them that hate me..." It is actually a statement of God's patience, and at the same time a declaration that the sins of a people have consequences. Think of it like this. The first generation is idolatrous (whether in action or in spirit), and seems to get by unscathed. They teach these values to their children, who teach them to their children, who teach them to their children. God will allow this for only so long. But in the third or fourth generation God will "visit" the situation. He will, so to speak, come down and have an inspection.

The consequences of idolatry are generational. Those who walk in disobedience to God are not necessarily visited in the immediate generation, but as the children learn and pass on the values, the end result is judgment; not just judgment on the last day, but the consequences of their sin comes upon them in history - in the history of that family or religion or nation or culture. The only way to break this pattern is through repentance and conversion - to turn from hating God to loving him. Then the story changes!

If God visits the iniquities of the fathers to the third and fourth generation of those who hate him, the commandment continues, "but showing love to a thousand {generations} of those who love me and keep my commandments", then here is the challenge to build a godly dynasty! You may have come from a family or a people who were idolatrous (maybe even from Christians who were idolatrous in their attempts to manipulate God). But you have changed that line, and instead of suffering the consequences of such ill-advised actions, you are now beginning to reap the benefits of loving God. *Pass it on to those who follow after you*!

A Thousand Generations

Let me interrupt this discussion for a soft little jab at people who are extremely literal when they read the Bible. Some people insist that when the Bible says seven days it *must* be interpreted as a literal seven days, or when it says a thousand years it *must* be interpreted as a literal thousand years. OK.

Fine. Let's do the math. Moses received this commandment from God in about the year 1500 B.C. If we are going to interpret this promise literally, and if a generation is about 40 years, then God will be faithful to those who love him for 40,000 years! If 3,500 years have already passed, then we have another 36,500 years to expect God's faithfulness. So much for the expectation of the immediate return of Christ! But, of course, I'm just having fun with the hyper-literalists who may be reading this book - my point is this: God is saying he will have mercy on *all* the generations that love him and keep his commandments.

If those who forsake God come to nothing every three or four generations, but those who love him and pass it on to their children just keep growing in the bounty and favor of God for a thousand generations, it becomes pretty clear who wins *in history* and in the end. Our expectations of the future should not be that the righteous will decline and need rescuing, but that the righteous will triumph! You see, I hope, just how important it is to think generationally about our faith in God. It is important not only for you to love God, but for you to teach your children and grandchildren to love him too.

So, No Statues In Church?

The nation of Israel pretty much broke this commandment on a regular basis, and it started a terrible cycle that is repeated throughout the Old Testament. First they would be delivered by God and enter into a season of prosperity and blessings, then they would grow lax in their faith and end up turning to idolatry. After a while in idolatry (maybe three or four generations), they would decline in favor, blessings and power, and be overrun by some oppressive regime (take your pick: Babylon, Assyria, Egypt, Rome). But after falling into captivity they would cry out to God who would raise up a deliverer for them, and they would return to that original state of blessing and favor. Then the cycle would repeat itself.

When the people of God went into captivity in Babylon (in the time of Daniel), they stayed there for seventy years. When they came back to the Promised Land, they completely swore off idols - even to the point of not having any statuary at all. No paintings of Grandmother on the walls of the house, and *certainly* no statues of angels, or Moses, or David. Later, the Muslim religion would take this same tack, forbidding the portrayal of any living beast.

Some Christians applaud this attitude - well, maybe not so far as to forbid pictures of Grandmother - but certainly to the point of saying there will be no use of statues or images in the Church. These folk look down their noses at Roman Catholics, Eastern Orthodox, and some Anglicans, seeing them as not much better than the idolaters of old.

Two things need to be said about this. First, in the Old Testament, images and statues were used in worship at practically every turn. In fact, God is the one who commanded their use!

- The basin for priestly cleansing was held up by statues of big bulls (2 Chronicles 4.1-5).

- The Ark of the Covenant had golden statues of cherubim (Exodus 25.17-22).

- The Curtain of the Holy of Holies had cherubim sown into the fabric (Exodus 26.31).

- The Holy of Holies had giant golden angels towering over it (2 Chronicles 3.10-13).

• The lampstand in the Temple looked like an almond tree (Exodus 25.31-36).

• The pillars of the Temple were fashioned as trees (2 Chronicles 3.5, 15-17).

• Moses made a bronze serpent which saved the people from poisonous snakebites (Numbers 21.8-9).

So, let's have none of this talk about not being able to use imagery in worship. The same God who said "don't bow down to idols" also said, "make me some golden angels and bulls".

But second, and more important, is the *change* which occurred in the incarnation, when God became man - when God joined himself to the stuff of his creation. Before the incarnation, it was impossible for men to describe, fully, what God was like. Any painting or statue of God would automatically be a less than adequate rendition. But when God became man in the person of Jesus Christ, he revealed, *in a physical form*, God's fullness! Saint John wrote, "The Word became flesh and made his dwelling among us. We have *seen* his glory, the glory of the One and Only, who came from the Father, full of grace and truth" (John 1.14). Later, John would also write, "That which was from the beginning, which we have *heard*, which we have *seen* with our eyes, which we have *looked at* and our hands have *touched* - this we proclaim concerning the Word of life" (1 John 1.1).

God forbade Israel to make an image of him, because they had not seen him:

> *You saw no form of any kind* the day
> the Lord spoke to you at Horeb out
> of the fire. *Therefore* watch
> yourselves very carefully, so that
> you do not become corrupt and
> make for yourselves an idol, an
> image of any shape, whether formed
> like a man or a woman, or like any
> animal on earth or any bird that flies
> in the air, or like any creature that
> moves along the ground or any fish
> in the waters below (Deuteronomy
> 4.15-18).

But with Christ, we *have* seen God!

It is important to understand that Jesus wasn't simply a *portrayal* of God, nor was he a manifestation of *part* of God. Paul tells us, "For in Christ *all the fullness* of the Deity lives in bodily form" (Colossians 2.9). "In bodily form" - God, in Christ, has become seeable, touchable - tangible.

In redeeming all creation - all "stuff", Christ has blessed the use of that stuff for worship, even beyond its use in the Old Testament. To bow before a cross is *not* idolatry. To reverence an image of Christ is *not* to worship a false God. These things can be abused (just like the bronze serpent was later turned into an idol), but the abuse of a thing does not invalidate its proper use.

Instead of judging our fellow Christians for using the very things the Bible commanded to be used (images and statues) in worshipping God, we should attend ourselves, and be sure that we do not live idolatrously, attempting to manipulate God for our own purposes. And as we follow him faithfully and seek first his kingdom, we should look for his blessings to be poured out upon us - for a thousand generations.

Chapter Three

You Shall Not Misuse God's Name

"You shall not misuse the name of the Lord your God, for the Lord will not hold anyone guiltless who misuses his name."

Back in the early part of the 20th century, when telephones were new and the automobile was just beginning to replace the horse and buggy, a con artist came up with a great scam. He secured a bunch of very cheap Bibles and a stamping machine to press names into the leather covers. Then he travelled from town to town reading the obituary columns. He would find a listing in the paper for someone who had died only days before, print his name on the cover of a Bible, then go knocking at the widow's door. "Is Mr. Robert Johnson here?", he would ask. When informed of Mr. Johnson's recent demise he would feign surprise and sorrow and then say, "I am so sorry to hear that. Well, he ordered this Bible with his name printed on it about four weeks ago, and I am here to deliver it, but we need not bother with that now. You have a good day..."

But of course, the con man would usually be stopped from leaving by a terribly surprised widow who thought her old croney of a husband might have secretly found religion in his final days. So the con man would reluctantly come back, and sell the Bible to the sentimental widow for about ten times what he had paid for it. Nice work if you can get it.

The art of conning is the art of *manipulation*. The third commandment is about not using God's name as a means of manipulation - either in an attempt to manipulate God, or to manipulate others.

Holy Is The Name Of The Lord

The first point of covenant declares that God is the transcendent one. He is completely unique and totally other. This, by the way, is the definition of the word "holy". When we declare that God is holy, we aren't making a statement about his morality (although all true morality flows from the reflection of his nature), we are stating that he is separate. Everything else, and I mean *everything*, is created, but he is the Creator. Everything else is finite, but he is infinite. Everything else exists conditionally - dependent on other factors - but he simply *is*; "I Am" is his name.

It should come as no surprise, then, that this unique God has a unique name. In the Old Testament, when Sampson's father, Manoah, encountered God and asked his name, the Lord replied, "Why do you ask my name? It is beyond understanding" (Judges 13.18).

When God revealed his name to Moses in Exodus 3, he called himself "I Am" - but the truth of the matter is, we don't know for sure what he said. Joy Davidman makes an insightful comment about this:

The city of Rome had a "real" name,
kept secret by the priests lest any
enemy learn it and use it for hostile
magic; kept secret so successfully
that we do not know it to this day.
The God of the Hebrews had a
"real" name, too full of power for
men to write it or speak it; for a
while only the high priest was
allowed to invoke it, once a year, in
the privacy of the Holy of Holies.
Eventually even he dared not utter
the sacred syllables, and so the
Name is lost to us - scholars have
spent fruitless years trying to
reconstruct it.[11]

What we *do* know are the consonants of
the name. We have lost the vowels. The
consonants are Y-H-W-H. So translators have
filled the gaps by writing it YaHWeH -
Yahweh, or YeHoWaH - Jehovah. Usually,
they just settle for "Lord" as a representative
word for the unutterable name. But the point
remains the same; to quote the Virgin Mary,
"for the Mighty One has done great things for
me - *holy is his name*" (Luke 1.45).

---

[11] Davidman, p. 41.

Ethics And The Name Of God

The first point of covenant is *transcendence*. The second point is *hierarchy*. Now we come to the third commandment and the third point of covenant: *ethics*. In a covenant document, the ethics section asks the question, "What are the rules?" After explaining who the High King of the covenant was, and who his representative hierarchy was, it finally got down to putting down on paper (or parchment, or stone), just what the rules were. Here was the meat of the covenant, the middle part.

Ethics has to do with proper and improper behavior, and the proper and improper use of things. Chief among all the things that God's people can lay hold of is that ineffable, unutterable, sacred, marvelous name by which he has made himself known, by which he has *revealed himself*. In traditional English, this commandment reads, "Thou shalt not take the name of the Lord [Yahweh] thy God in vain". You shall not use it in an *empty* way. Joy Davidman points out that this, "is a misleading phrase to modern ears, for the original point was that one *couldn't* take it in vain, in our sense. That is, if one called on God by his right name, however casually, things started to happen!" She continues, "Thus the Third Commandment is not just a nice-Nellyish warning against profanity. It is much more like the sort of warning you see around power plants: 'Danger - High Voltage!'[12]

How Is God's Name Misused?

All this brings us to the application of the commandment in our own lives. How is it possible to misuse God's name? I will suggest several ways, beginning with the most obvious (and least significant).

Profanity: We live in an age where nearly every book, movie and television program portrays the misuse of God's name in profanity. It has become so commonplace to us that many Christians find it falling out of their own lips without thought.

When it comes to profanity in general, I would argue that the great majority of profane words are culturally established, and they change with the evolution of the culture. Some words that were scandalous a hundred years ago are commonly accepted now, and some words we find abhorrent now were part of common speech a century ago. Although the

---

[12] Davidman, p. 42f.

Bible does tell us to be careful about using vulgar language, such language truly is conditional and has to be addressed in context.

When my son was studying linguistics in college we often had long and interesting discussions about language, and one was about how vulgar words become vulgar words. More times than not it is because the language of a conquered or oppressed people becomes uncouth in ruling upper class circles, and so many if not most of our curse words are just the old-time common words for a thing, whereas if we spoke of the same matter in the language of the upper class it would be perfectly suitable to mixed company and cultured gatherings. "Piss", for example, is a good English word used in the Bible, but now thought of as crude (cf. 1 Samuel 25.22, 34; 1 Kings 14.10, Isaiah 36.12, KJV, for a few of the many examples).

But to use God's name in common (vulgar, by the way, simply means common) speech is another thing. Modern people have lost the distinction between the sacred and the common. Among the ancients, things, people, places, and language were set aside as special to God. In fact, God told Moses to, "tell Aaron and his sons to *treat with respect* the *sacred offerings* the Israelites consecrate to me, *so they will not profane my holy name*. I am the Lord" (Leviticus 22.2). The common use of sacred things was seen as a profaning of God's name, how much more the common use of his sacred name!

Cursing: To say "God damn you" sounds like profanity. It isn't. It is cursing. There is a difference. Profanity is the use of uncouth words, and the misuse of God's name in common conversation. Cursing is invoking the wrath of God on someone unjustly. To say, "God damn you" is shorthand for saying, I pronounce the eternal damnation of God upon your soul." Likewise, "Go to hell" is invoking a punishment that only God himself is authorized to deliver. Interestingly, even the civil government, when meting out the death penalty, never condemns the soul to hell, but simply the body to the grave. The words that usually follow are, "May God have mercy on your soul."

Manipulation: Now we come to a breaking of the third commandment that is much more subtle and dangerous. Manipulation is an attempt to invoke God's power or use his name to accomplish some natural or supernatural end which is not in keeping with his will. Manipulation comes in two forms, magical and natural.

Magical manipulation is seen when Satanists or Voodoo practitioners use the name of God in their ceremonies to control the demonic presence or to bring curses on others. It is also seen when people, Christians included, use God's name in prayer while praying foolishly and selfishly without being willing to submit their will to God's will. As an extreme example, imagine someone going up to the altar of the church, kneeling down, and praying that God kill his wife so he can marry his lover, and finishing, "In Jesus' name". To even think that this is legitimate prayer is foolish, but it also becomes a magical incantation when the person assumes that simply naming the name of God somehow puts God to work on their evil behalf.

An example of natural manipulation is when a salesman tells a customer that he is a Christian and can be trusted, all the while planning to unload a defective item on the unsuspecting client. It happens all the time in business, and every time it happens it is a breaking of the third commandment.

Improper Oaths: In the Sermon on the Mount, Jesus said,

Again, you have heard that it was said to the people long ago, "Do not break your oath, but keep the oaths you have made to the Lord." But I tell you, Do not swear at all: either by heaven, for it is God's throne; or by the earth, for it is his footstool; or by Jerusalem, for it is the city of the Great King. And do not swear by your head, for you cannot make even one hair white or black. Simply let your "Yes" be "Yes," and your "No," "No"; anything beyond this comes from the evil one (Matthew 5.33-37).

When a person swears on the Bible, or by God's name ("May God strike me dead if I'm lying!"), and then is unfaithful to the promise made, he has misused God's name. When he is not immediately judged by God (because of God's grace), then God's power and justice have been brought into question. Jesus taught that believers should not make oaths in every day life. There are proper oaths to be made (and I should point out that true covenants always contain oaths). But these are made only in the context of the covenant authorities established by God - the family, the Church, and the civil government.

Breaking Proper Oaths: When a person makes a legitimate oath, in the name of God, and then breaks it, he is misusing God's name.

Making Proper Oaths

The three covenant institutions established by God - the family, the Church, and civil authority - each possess the rightful use of *sanctions* (the fourth point of covenant) in the establishment of covenant. In these contexts, oaths are not only permitted, they are expected. Biblically, oaths are a swearing of allegiance to the covenant ethics, and an invoking of the sanctions if the ethics are not fulfilled.

Family: When a man and a woman are joined together in marriage, they are making a covenant before God. The covenant involves ethics (godly behavior toward one another), and sanctions (both blessings and curses). The covenant is then sealed with an oath (a vow), which ends, "till death do us part". Properly understood, the oath is calling on God to deliver the judgment of death on the party that breaches the covenant!

Church: When a person is baptized into the Body of Christ, an oath is acted out in word and action. The person affirms their faith in Christ, and renounces all their allegiances to Satan and his forces. What is symbolized is the burying of one's own will and one's sinful nature, and the resurrection of that person into a new life in Christ Jesus. The baptism is performed, "*in the name* of the Father, and of the Son, and of the Holy Spirit". Baptism is an oath that the person will be faithful to the covenant being made with God and his people. It says, in so many words, "My old life is dead. It doesn't exist anymore. So if I reject this covenant of grace and forsake Christ, I acknowledge this day that I am returning to nothing but death. I am invoking death - both physically and spiritually - if this covenant is abandoned."

Civil Government: When the civil government courts call a person as a witness, an oath in God's name is often demanded: "I swear to tell the truth, the whole truth, and nothing but the truth, so help me God". Even if the name of God is not verbally invoked, for a Christian to take this oath at all is an invoking of God's name, for God's name has already been invoked over the whole life of the believer. To lie, or perjure one's self, is to break an oath made before God. Under Old Testament biblical law, the penalty for perjury was to receive the punishment that would have been brought upon the victim of the perjury (cf. Deuteronomy 19.16-21). Although that penalty is not meted out in our time, to swear by God's name is to invoke the penalty of judgment if we swear falsely.

The point I am trying to make is that our words are powerful weapons that can be used to bring about blessings or curses in our lives. They should not be spoken hastily, either in oath-making or in any other context. And when our words include *the* Word - the name of God, the name of Jesus, we should be particularly careful.

The name of God is holy. It is sacred, set apart. It should never be misused by believers. But it *should* be used! It should be used in blessing, in praise, and at every opportunity we have to glorify that wonderful name.

Chapter Four

Keep The Sabbath

"Remember the Sabbath day by keeping it holy. Six days you shall labor and do all your work, but the seventh day is a Sabbath to the Lord your God. On it you shall not do any work, neither you, nor your son or daughter, nor your manservant or maidservant, nor your animals, nor the alien within your gates. For in six days the Lord made the heavens and the earth, the sea, and all that is in them, but he rested on the seventh day. Therefore the Lord blessed the Sabbath day and made it holy."

"Keep the Sabbath holy" conjures up negative images for a lot of Christians. The legalistic shutting down of everything fun, dour faces staring judgmentally if you smiled on the Lord's Day, and if you lived in Texas or somewhere similar, the famous "blue laws" which forbade the sale of anything except the bare essentials on Sunday. Before we go any further with the subject, let me set your mind at ease. This chapter is not about being a killjoy one day a week. It is, instead, about a day of *rejoicing*. Joy Davidman asked the question, "How does one keep a day holy? By making it unpleasant, and restrictive, and boring - or by making it joyous? By making it as much as possible like hell, or as much as possible like heaven?"[13]

The fourth commandment follows logically from the first three. J.I. Packer writes, "The underlying principle is clear - namely, that we must honor God not only by our loyalty (first commandment) and thought-life (second commandment) and words (third commandment), but also by our use of time..."[14] This next commandment is about setting aside time to glorify God.

---

[13] Davidman, p. 52.

[14] Packer, p. 67.

Blessings and Curses

The fourth point of covenant is *sanctions*. It asks the question, "What are the consequences of keeping the rules or breaking the rules?" The fourth commandment is clearly a commandment related to sanctions. The text says, "Therefore the Lord *blessed* the Sabbath day and made it holy".

As with the rest of the first five commandments, this one has both a command and a reason for the command. The command is "remember the Sabbath day by keeping it holy" - we will talk more about how to do this in due course. But first notice the two reasons given for keeping a Sabbath.

In the Exodus 20 account of the giving of the Ten Commandments (the one we are referencing the most in this book), we are told that the Sabbath rest is a blessing tied directly with creation. God rested on the seventh day, and he established a principle for his people to rest too.

There is an additional reason given in the Deuteronomy 5 telling of the commandments:

Observe the Sabbath day by keeping it holy, as the Lord your God has commanded you. Six days you shall labor and do all your work, but the seventh day is a Sabbath to the Lord your God...*Remember that you were slaves in Egypt and that the Lord your God brought you out of there with a mighty hand and an outstretched arm. Therefore* the Lord your God has commanded you to observe the Sabbath day (Deuteronomy 5.12-15).

Not only is the Sabbath honored because of the rhythm of God's work and rest in creation, it is also honored as a symbol of Israel being a *free people*. Slaves don't get a day of rest. In Egypt the people didn't get to enjoy a Sabbath. Nor were they free to worship God in the weekly routine which he mandated from the time of creation. The Sabbath, then, was a kind of luxury, a sign of affluence and blessing. Literally, the word means "intermission" - a break from work.

In observing the Sabbath the people were to remember that God was their Creator, but he was also their *Deliverer*. He had delivered them from slavery in Egypt. In the same way, Christians honor the Lord's Day (more about the change in days later), because they have been set free from the bondage of sin and death, and because - and this is very important - they are resting, not only from their own labors, but in the *finished work* of Christ! Ready for another long passage of Scripture that I'm going to insist you read carefully? OK, here is an amazing passage from the book of Hebrews. Pay particular attention to the italicized verses (but don't just skip down and read those alone. I mean it. I'm watching!):

> Therefore, since the promise of entering his rest still stands, let us be careful that none of you be found to have fallen short of it. For we also have had the gospel preached to us, just as they did; but the message they heard was of no value to them, because those who heard did not combine it with faith. Now we who have believed enter that rest, just as God has said, "So I declared an oath in my anger, 'They shall never enter my rest.'" And yet his work has been finished since the creation of the world. For somewhere he has spoken about the seventh day in these words: "And on the seventh day God rested from all his work."

And again in the passage above he says, "They shall never enter my rest."

It still remains that some will enter that rest, and those who formerly had the gospel preached to them did not go in, because of their disobedience. Therefore God again set a certain day, calling it Today, when a long time later he spoke through David, as was said before: "Today, if you hear his voice, do not harden your hearts." For if Joshua had given them rest, God would not have spoken later about another day. *There remains, then, a Sabbath-rest for the people of God; for anyone who enters God's rest also rests from his own work, just as God did from his.* Let us, therefore, make every effort to enter that rest, so that no one will fall by following their example of disobedience. (Hebrews 4.1-11).

Paul said it much more simply: "For it is by grace you have been saved...not by works" (Ephesians 2.8-9).

The *Rest* Of The Story

The Sabbath - the Intermission - is all about resting. Resting is a positive sanction, a blessing, of keeping the covenant. In Genesis we read that God created man on the sixth day, actually at the *end* of the sixth day. Man was the last thing on God's to-do list. You have probably heard the story about the first day of creation, when God told the angels that he had just created a 24 hour period of time made half of daylight and half of darkness. One of the angels responded, "Great! Now what are you going to do?" And God said, "I think I'll call it a day". But when God finished with his masterpiece, Adam and Eve, he *did* call it a day. He was done with work, now it was time for rest.

This is where it gets complicated and you have to focus. You may be tempted to glaze over as you read these next few paragraphs, and I completely understand, but please give it a shot.

When God finished with the creation of humanity, he was done with it all. He rested on the seventh day. God's rest was a result of his work. You might say, he *earned* his rest. But God's *seventh* day was man's *first* day. Adam and Eve were called to join God in *his* rest on *their* first day, signifying, you have probably figured out by now, them enjoying the finished work of God, not their own finished work. They hadn't done *any* work yet and here they were being called by God to take a day off!

In short, God was telling Adam and Eve to rest in his completed work. Here's a question for you: how long do you think Adam and Eve hung around before they got to that apple-eating bit of the story? Decades? Years? Months? Weeks? No one knows for sure, but the old rabbis taught that they bit the fruit on the very day they were supposed to be chilling out. "Hey, Eve, we have the day off, want to go for a walk in the park?" "Sure, Adam, hey, doesn't that apple look delicious?" And so, what began as a day of *blessing* became instead a day of *cursing*, when God's judgment was delivered to Adam, Eve, the serpent and the earth itself.

The seventh day Sabbath, therefore, became a sign of both blessing and cursing. It became a sign of covenant *sanctions*. In the Old Testament the Sabbath day spoke of both blessing and cursing, but it spoke primarily of cursing. The Old Testament day of rest was indeed on the seventh day - but not on God's seventh day, rather on *man's seventh day*. It was indeed a day of blessing in that it provided rest, but it was a day of cursing in this: by resting on man's seventh day the people were declaring that they could not rest in God's finished work. They were leaning on their *own* abilities. They were resting from their *own* labors. They were under the curse of Adam and were looking forward to when Jesus Christ would come and reverse the curse and set things right that had gone wrong.

The First Day Of The Week

According to the Scriptures, Jesus was crucified for the sins of mankind, and then rose from the dead "on the first day of the week" (what we would call Sunday) (Matthew 28.1, Mark 16.1,2, Luke 24.1, John 20.1). Since then, Christians have gathered to worship God, not on the seventh day, but on the first day of the week (Acts 20.7, 1 Corinthians 16.2). Two important changes took place.

First, God's special day was no longer referred to as the Sabbath, but as "The Lord's Day" (Revelation 1.10).

Second, Whereas in the Old Testament the primary emphasis of the Sabbath was rest and the secondary emphasis was worship, in the New Testament the primary emphasis of the Lord's Day is worship, with a secondary emphasis on rest.

We see, then, that the Old Testament Sabbath expectation of the day when God's people could rest in his finished work was fulfilled in Jesus Christ. The curse has been lifted and the blessing has been expanded. Saint Paul wrote, "Therefore do not let anyone judge you by what you eat or drink, or with regard to a religious festival, a New Moon celebration or a Sabbath day. These are a shadow of the things that were to come; the reality, however, is found in Christ" (Colossians 2.16-17).

Let me say it one more time, clearly, just to make sure that you get it: God's seventh day is man's first day. Jesus rose on man's first day (God's seventh day). Sunday worship and rest is a restoration of the pre-fall calendar. We are still called to honor a day of the Lord, it has just been returned to it's rightful schedule.

How Do We Keep A Day Holy?

Now that we've taken care of that complicated bit of calendar adjustment, we are still left with the question of how we "keep" a day holy.

Honoring the Sabbath has been given a bad rap by legalists, from the time of Jesus right down to our own day. The Pharisees were sticklers for what was and was not breaking the Sabbath. They claimed dragging a chair across the dirt floor of a kitchen was breaking the Sabbath because it was "plowing". They said you couldn't wear false teeth on the sabbath because they might fall out, and you would have to pick them up, and that would be carrying a burden. Here's my favorite - they said it was breaking the Sabbath if you picked up a rock, but it wasn't breaking the Sabbath if you picked up your child. But you should probably play it safe and *not* pick up your child, just in case he had a rock in his hand! One Sabbath day they saw Jesus plucking a handful of grain and eating it, and they accused him of breaking the Sabbath because he was harvesting on that sacred day (Matthew 12.1,2). Jesus was often accused of violating the Sabbath, but he never did. He simply ignored the legalistic barnacles that had accumulated over the years, and he restored the proper use of the Sabbath by saying, "The Sabbath was made for man, not man for the Sabbath" (Mark 2.27).

Sadly, many who have followed after Jesus and named him as their Lord have acted much more like the Pharisees than like Jesus. The story is told of a Scottish pastor from the 19th century who found the roads blocked with snow one wintry Sunday morning and was forced to skate on the frozen river to get to church, which he did. When he arrived the elders of the church were horrified that their preacher had skated on the Lord's Day. After the service they held a meeting where the pastor explained that it was either skate to church or not go at all. Finally one elder asked, "Well, did you *enjoy* it?" When the preacher answered, "No," the board decided it was all right!

Please allow me to offer a few tips on truly honoring a Sabbath day, the Lord's day.

First, make it a priority to worship. The ancient Jews kept the Sabbath as a reminder that they were freed from the bondage of Egypt. We should honor the Lord's day in celebration of the day of his Resurrection - the day we were liberated from the curse of sin. There is no greater way to keep this day holy than to be in the house of God, with the people of God, celebrating with thanksgiving the victory won for us in Christ. Intentionally worshipping God on the Lord's Day should be of highest priority in the life of the believer.

Second, make it a day of rest as much as possible. Some people are required to work on Sunday. This is an unfortunate reality, but it is also, in a small way, a curse of poverty. Let me explain. If a Christian were independently wealthy, or could simply say, "No!" to an employer without risking livelihood, then worshipping on Sunday with God's people would not even be an issue for them. It is because they are under the hand of another that they must work on this day.

If at all possible, make this day a day of worship and a day of rest. Spend time relaxing, doing good deeds for others, in fellowship with friends or family. After worshipping God, make the rest of the day *different* from every other day of the week.

Finally, and I say this with all sincerity, *enjoy yourself*! Joy Davidman wrote of the Old Covenant Sabbath,

> On this one day, man returned to Eden. The curse of Adam was lifted, the primal Fall undone somewhat, and all creatures caught a glimmering of the paradisial state in

which everything God had made was very good. On this one day a man was commanded to enjoy himself."[15]

The Lord's Day is the chief day we celebrate the Lord's Supper - the Lord's Feast. It is a foretaste of that one Eternal Day we look forward to which begins with our own resurrection. Jesus said "The kingdom of heaven is like a...banquet" (Matthew 22.2). He also said, "Blessed is the man who will eat at the *feast of the kingdom of God*" (Luke 14.15). If the Lord's Day is a glimpse of the great feast day to come, it should be more like a fiesta than anything else.

Let the party begin!

---

[15] Davidman, p. 53.

Chapter Five

Honor Your Father And Your Mother

"Honor your father and your mother, so that you may live long in the land the Lord your God is giving you."

One day, a while after that recent unpleasantness of the flood which had so disrupted his life, Noah planted a vineyard, grew some grapes, and made some wine. He was, after all, a farmer by trade. Then he decided that, what with having just come through a deluge of cataclysmic proportions, and what with having spent all those months cooped up with those obnoxious animals, and what with being one of only eight survivors anywhere to be seen, and what with having to start life over from scratch, he needed a drink.

So he poured himself a nice smooth merlot, and sat down in his comfortable recliner. After flipping through the channels and finding nothing worth watching on the television, he started reflecting on all he had been through. "Someone should write a book about this," he said to himself, "but people would probably think it a myth!" And as he thought, he sipped. And sipped. And sipped. Never realizing that, what with having just come through a deluge of cataclysmic proportions, and what with having spent all those months cooped up with those obnoxious animal, and what with being one of only eight survivors anywhere to be seen, and what with having to start life over from scratch, he hadn't had any alcohol in his system for years. It went straight to his head, and he laid down in his tent to sleep it off. Naked.

Now, Noah had three grown sons, Ham, Shem and Japheth, who had all gone on the big boat ride with him. The morning after the winefest, the oldest son walked into Daddy's tent and saw him in his state of naked hangover. Ham, always being, well, a ham, went running to his brothers laughing about what he had seen and exposing his father's nakedness. Horrified, Shem and Japheth found a blanket, walked *backwards* into the tent, and covered their father, never seeing him in his embarrassing condition.

When Noah came to his senses, he cursed Ham and blessed the other sons. I think Ham said something like, "Why are you cursing me? The fifth commandment won't be written for centuries!" But of course, the principle of honoring your parents didn't start with Moses on Sinai. It has always been the bedrock of the family, and of civilization itself. God just told Moses to write it down.

As with the rest of the first five commandments, the fifth has both a command and a reason for the command. The command is "honor your father and your mother". The reason is "that you may live long in the land the Lord your God is giving you." The second version adds, "and that it may go well with you" (Deuteronomy 5.16).

Covenant Continuity

The fifth commandment correlates to the fifth point of biblical covenant, *continuity*. The question asked in this section of the covenant is, "How can this covenant be extended and continued?" The very first place that covenant is established and continued is in the context of family life. The Church has always recognized the family as being "the domestic Church" - the place where faith in God is birthed and nurtured even in the youngest members of the family. J.I. Packer wrote,

> What we must realize is that God, who is himself a father - the Father of our Lord Jesus Christ and of all Christians through him - cares about families enormously. Family life, with its built-in responsibilities for both parents and children, is part of his purpose for all, and the way we behave as children and parents is a prime test of both our humanity and our godliness.[16]

When the Apostle Paul wrote to Timothy, he recognized the source of Timothy's faith in God: "I have been reminded of your sincere faith, which first lived in your grandmother Lois and in your mother Eunice and, I am persuaded, now lives in you also" (2 Timothy 1.5).

---

[16] Packer, p. 73.

Saint Paul, who actually wrote quite a bit about family relationships, saw the family as the center of civilization, and recognized the breakdown of the family as one of he signs of a decaying culture. Writing to the Christians in Rome, where the culture was at a point of collapse, he lists a long litany of horrible conditions:

> They have become filled with every kind of wickedness, evil, greed and depravity. They are full of envy, murder, strife, deceit and malice. They are gossips, slanderers, God-haters, insolent, arrogant and boastful; they invent ways of doing evil...

Then he adds this: *"they disobey their parents"* (Romans 1.29-30).

In another place, when he describes to Timothy the awful conditions he saw around him, he gives another long list of indicators of societal collapse, describing the people as

> lovers of themselves, lovers of money, boastful, proud, abusive, *disobedient to their parents*, ungrateful, unholy, without love, unforgiving, slanderous, without self-control,

117

brutal, not lovers of the good,
treacherous, rash, conceited, lovers
of pleasure rather than lovers of
God - having a form of godliness but
denying its power" (2 Timothy
3.2-5).

The breakdown of the family and the breaking
of the fifth commandment were so significant
to the Apostle that he added it to the likes of
murder, brutality and treachery!

By honoring parents, a generation
receives the *inheritance* of the parents (the
positive sanction, or blessing, of the family),
both materially and spiritually. The covenant
is continued into the next generation as are the
blessings of the covenant. In her book *Lifelines*,
Edith Schaeffer shows the "naturalness" of the
fifth commandment and its promise:

> The promise to the Israelites as they
> began to live in the land that God
> had given to them was that the
> careful continuity of possessing,
> farming, caring for, and living on a
> piece of land would be a family
> heritage for generations. Being truly
> human involves family relationships
> with, first of all, the child-parent
> relationship, and then the continuity

of a "homestead", a place, a piece of
terrain, a piece of land, an acre, a
garden and house...By binding
together the law with a promise,
God showed what He meant by the
peaceful life He wanted for His
children, if they would follow His
law and live by His word.[17]

In order for a godly covenant to
continue, unbroken from one generation to
another and then another, there are
responsibilities both for the older generation
and the younger.

Parent-To-Child Responsibilities

Before there can be any talk of children
honoring their parents, the parents have
responsibilities to the children. They must
raise them as children of honor.

The first parent-to-child responsibility
is to *train the child* in the covenant, that is, in
godliness. Solomon in his wisdom wrote,
"Train a child in the way he should go, and
when he is old he will not turn from
it" (Proverbs 22.6). In other words, a child

[17] Schaeffer, Edith, *Lifelines - The Ten Commandments For
Today*, Westchester, Ill, Crossway Books, 1982, p. 104.

must be taught who God is (*transcendence*), to respect and obey authority (*hierarchy*), to keep the rules for right living (*ethics*), that there are consequences to the choices we make (*sanctions*), and to pass what they have received on to their own children (*continuity*). This is made even more obvious in Moses' words to the people of Israel in Deuteronomy:

These are the commands, decrees and laws the Lord your God directed me to teach you to observe in the land that you are crossing the Jordan to possess, *so that you, your children and their children after them* may fear the Lord your God as long as you live by keeping all his decrees and commands that I give you, and so that you *may enjoy long life [compare this with the promise of the fifth commandment in Exodus 20.12]*. Hear, O Israel, and be careful to obey so that it may *go well with you [compare this with the promise of the fifth commandment in Deuteronomy 5.16]* and that you may increase greatly *[How does a family or nation increase greatly? Through faithful offspring.]* in a land flowing with milk and honey, just as the Lord, the God of your fathers, promised you.

Hear, O Israel: The Lord our God, the Lord is one. Love the Lord your God with all your heart and with all your soul and with all your strength. These commandments that I give you today are to be upon your hearts. *Impress them on your children.* Talk about them when you sit at home and when you walk along the road, when you lie down and when you get up. Tie them as symbols on your hands and bind them on your foreheads. Write them on the doorframes of your houses and on your gates.

When the Lord your God brings you into the land he swore to your fathers, to Abraham, Isaac and Jacob, to give you — a land with large, flourishing cities you did not build, houses filled with all kinds of good things you did not provide, wells you did not dig, and vineyards and olive groves you did not plant - then when you eat and are satisfied, be careful that you do not forget the Lord, who brought you out of Egypt, out of the land of slavery (Deuteronomy 6.1-12).

Again, Edith Schaeffer:

The command to respect and honor
mother and father is very carefully
tied in with both mother and father
respecting the law of God, not
forgetting to teach their children,
and encouraging them by answering
their questions...The failure to give
either true teaching or right example
to children makes the father and
mother a detriment to the next
generation. Sadly, this breaks or rips
up the pattern that is meant to be
handed down and protected.[18]

Another parent-to-child responsibility is
to *lay up an inheritance* for the children.
Solomon said, "A good man leaves an
inheritance for his children's children, but a
sinner's wealth is stored up for the
righteous" (Proverbs 13.22). As the righteous
prosper under the hand of God, they should
not squander their increased goods, but should
lay them up for future generations to build
upon. Over a period of time this results in
developing *godly dynasties* which are influential
in all spheres of life. Inheritance refers not

---

[18] *ibid*, p. 105f.

only to monetary gain, but also to skills, traditions, land, and heritage.

I know a wealthy man who made out his will to leave most of what he has to his church denomination and only a significantly smaller portion to his children and grandchildren. I'm sure he thought he was acting in a spiritual manner, but I believe he completely missed the spiritual significance of the family. When Saint Paul was about to visit the Christians in Corinth, he wrote, "Now I am ready to visit you for a third time, and I will not be a burden to you. After all, *children should not have to save up for their parents, but parents for their children*" (2 Corinthians 12.14). Contrast Paul's attitude with that of many modern media-ministers who encourage supporters to will them their inheritance instead of leaving it for the family! Notice also what Jesus said to the Pharisees:

> And why do you break the command of God for the sake of your tradition? For God said, Honor your father and mother" and "Anyone who curses his father or mother must be put to death." But you say that if a man says to his father or mother, "Whatever help you might otherwise have received

from me is a gift devoted to God,"
he is not to "honor his father" with
it. Thus you nullify the word of God
for the sake of your tradition
(Matthew 15.3-6).

Child-To-Parent Responsibilities

In addition to parents having
responsibilities to raise their children in the
faith and provide them with a godly
inheritance, children also have responsibilities
toward their parents, and this is the crux of
the fifth commandment.

The first child-to-parent responsibility
is to *honor the parents*. By honoring parents, the
younger generation keeps the values and
traditions passed on to them from previous
generations. They remain faithful to their
parents' covenant with God, making it their
own covenant as well. A few years ago I met a
priest in the Antiochian Orthodox Church. He
lives in the United States now, but was born in
Lebanon. What impressed me about him was
not his beautiful and large new church, nor his
obvious knowledge of the faith. What
impressed me was that he was an eleventh
generation Orthodox priest! Talk about
continuity! He had honored his father and

kept the faith, and the blessing of God was upon him.

To do the opposite - to dishonor our parents - means to be cut off from the inheritance (both spiritually and physically), and thus cut off from "the land". When this happens there is no "long life in the land" - the society begins to fall into chaos and eventually succumbs to outside powers. It has happened again and again in the history of the world, but it also happens on a smaller scale in individual family life. Once again, Edith Schaeffer makes a valuable comment concerning the *practical ways* we can honor one another:

> How often do we cook special food, take baskets of fruit, pick flowers and arrange them, knit sweaters or shawls, make clothing, provide vacations, send books or chocolates, send grapefruit or apples in season...How much do we think about how we can provide for our family or relatives? We are worse than unbelievers if we do not, so we are told.[19]

---

[19] *ibid*, p. 108.

Another child-to-parent responsibility is to *care for the parents in their years of need*. Paul wrote to Timothy, "If anyone does not provide for his relatives, and especially for his immediate family, he has denied the faith and is worse than an unbeliever" (1 Timothy 5.8). After providing for children and even grandchildren through the prime of life, there may come a time when parents need provision themselves. Often it is not so much monetary provision as emotional support and simply being there for them. In previous generations, houses were built with the intention of grandparents living with the family in their old age. This is something we have tragically lost in modern times and should seek to recover. In settings like this older parents can be honored with love and attention from younger generations.

The First Commandment With Promise

When Saint Paul was writing the Church in Ephesus about how to live as Christians, he penned, "Children, obey your parents in the Lord, for this is right. 'Honor your father and mother - *which is the first commandment with a promise* - 'that it may go well with you and that you may enjoy long life on the earth'" (Ephesians 6.1-3). This means two things.

It means that a family or a culture as a whole which honors its older generations will long endure in the land. By honoring our parents, continuity is established and a family or culture is strengthened against both internal decay and external attack.

It also means that the specific generations of that family or culture can expect to have longer life spans. There will be a progressive expansion of life expectancy in the generations.

Couple this promise with the implications of the second commandment - that those who are righteous will be blessed for a thousand generations but the wicked will be visited with judgment in three or four! Where the covenant is kept and passed on, where the Commandments are honored, victory, peace and blessings are the inevitable outcome.

As an aside, this brings up another interesting question. How long is "long" as it relates to the fifth commandment? What would you say is a long life span? I watched an episode of a television detective show recently, where the brilliant investigator was trying to solve the murder of the oldest man in the world. The man was days away from being 115 years old and had been killed by a ruthless killer. When the investigator interviewed the 85 year old son of the victim, the son broke down crying and said, "115 is too young to die!" Funny! But how old should a person live to be? 90? 120? 500? Just as a thought provoker, read what the prophet Isaiah said about the reversal of the curse which began with the arrival of the Messiah:

> Never again will there be in it an infant who lives but a few days, or an old man who does not live out his years; *he who dies at a hundred will be thought a mere youth; he who fails to reach a hundred will be considered accursed*. They will build houses and dwell in them; they will plant vineyards and eat their fruit. No longer will they build houses and others live in them, or plant and others eat. For as the days of a tree, so will be the days of my people; my chosen ones will *long enjoy* the works of their hands. They will not toil in vain or bear children doomed to misfortune; for they will be a people blessed by the Lord, they and their descendants with them (Isaiah 65.20-23).

Maybe the 85 year old grieving son in the television program was right - 115 is too young to die!

Enemies Of Strong Families

Finally, it should be noted that there are enemies to strong families. It seems that the primary enemy to strong families in our modern time is unrighteous civil government. Many times governments legislate laws which are detrimental to strong, healthy, moral, godly families. Joy Davidman makes a prescient observation about modern society as an enemy of the family:

> Everybody today - Fascists and Communists and all of us in-betweens - will agree that family life is indispensable to human health and happiness. yet we find ourselves accepting conditions that make war on the family. The lands behind the Iron Curtain deliberately weaken ties in their schools, lest loyalty to parents should conflict with devotion to the sacred State. Our own country tries to keep the home fires burning with verbal sentiment about Mom, but meanwhile forces

Mom to leave the hearth fire untended while she tends the factory machine. A century ago, American houses were twelve-room affairs designed to hold grandparents, and maiden aunts, and uncles, as well as parents and children; today they are usually cramped little flats and cottages, and we feel lucky to get those. We can hardly do much about honoring Father and Mother if there's no room for them in the inn...Clear heads among us do this for themselves - there are plenty of "child-centered homes" even today. What stops the rest of us? An airy nothing, a climate of opinion, a complacent belief that things are all right as they are, that civilization and progress consist in having the State do as much as possible and the home as little as possible - in short, that the less family life we have, the better.[20]

These words were penned in 1953! How much more do we see the civil government attempting to replace the family in our own day, in the areas of education,

---

[20] Davidman, p. 63f.

welfare, social security, etc.? How much more do we see our own culture drawing us away from family and toward selfish individuality? We must constantly be aware of the things that threaten our family structures and defend our families from them. We can start by honoring our fathers and our mothers.

Perhaps the final word should be left to that wise old Jewish sage, Jesus Ben Sirach, who wrote two hundred years before the birth of Christ:

> Children, pay heed to a father's
> right; do so that you may live.
>
> For the Lord sets a father in honor
> over his children; a mother's
> authority he confirms over her sons.
>
> He who honors his father atones for
> sins; he stores up riches who reveres
> his mother.
>
> He who honors his father is
> gladdened by children, and when he
> prays he is heard.
>
> He who reveres his father will live a
> long life; he obeys the Lord who
> brings comfort to his mother.

He who fears the Lord honors his
father, and serves his parents as
rulers.

In word and deed honor your father
that his blessing may come upon
you;

For a father's blessing gives a family
firm roots, but a mother's curse
uproots the growing plant.

Glory not in your father's shame, for
his shame is no glory to you!

His father's honor is a man's glory;
disgrace for her children, a mother's
shame.

My son, take care of your father
when he is old; grieve him not as
long as he lives.

Even if his mind fail, be considerate
with him; revile him not in the
fullness of your strength.

For kindness to a father will not be
forgotten, it will serve as a sin
offering--it will take lasting root.

In time of tribulation it will be recalled to your advantage, like warmth upon frost it will melt away your sins (Ecclesiasticus 3.2-15).

Chapter Six

You Shall Not Kill

"You shall not murder."

Killing innocent people isn't anything new. It has been around as long as - well, as long as Cain, who murdered his brother Abel in the fourth chapter of Genesis. Killing with religion as its basis isn't anything new either. It has been around since Cain and Abel too.

With the sixth commandment, we begin the covenant cycle over again. Although the text says, "You shall not kill", no one applies this commandment to cockroaches or weeds.

We all understand that it refers to the taking of human life - because human life is *different*.

In The Image Of God

The first point of covenant is *transcendence*, and it asks the question, "Who makes the rules?" or, "Who is in charge?" The answer, we have already seen, is, "God is the one in charge. He makes he rules".

The reason God forbids the taking of human life is because human life is made in the image of God. "So God created man in his own image, in the image of God he created him; male and female he created them" (Genesis 1.27). Human beings, who are the pinnacle, the head, of creation, are indeed God's hierarchy in creation - his representatives, but more significantly, we portray God's transcendence to all creation. To kill an innocent person is an act of rebellion against that person's Creator whom he represents. The sixth commandment is a directive against destroying God's transcendent image found in mankind.

A Unique Creature

Mankind is unique among all creation because he was created in the image of God. A more detailed account of that creation is found in the second chapter of Genesis, where we read that "the Lord God formed the man from the dust of the ground and breathed into his nostrils the breath of life, and the man became a living being" (Genesis 2.7). In both Hebrew (*ruach*) and Greek (*pneuma*), the word *breath* is identical with the word *spirit*. The breath that God breathed into man was the "Spirit of life" - his own Spirit.

Mankind was the pinnacle of creation. Throughout the various acts of creation God became progressively more involved. With the plant and animal life, he simply said, "let the land produce vegetation...[and] living creatures..." (Genesis 1.11,24). But when it came time for humanity, God himself "got his hands dirty". He became intimately involved in this act, and gave life to the clay-formed body by breathing his own Spirit into it.

The life possessed by mankind is superior to all other created life. It is a life that flows from the very person of God. *That life in itself* is uniquely connected to the transcendent Lord, and is therefore holy.

God's Command To Noah

Mount Sinai is not the first place we learn that the taking of innocent human life is immoral. After the world had been destroyed by the flood, when Noah and his family set out to create not only a new family, but a new civilization, God said to Noah, "And from each man, too, I will demand an accounting for the life of his fellow man. Whoever sheds the blood of man, by man shall his blood be shed; for in the image of God has God made man" (Genesis 9.5-6).

Two things can be seen in this instruction to Noah. First, as we have already noted, man is forbidden from taking another's life because all mankind is made in the image of God and therefore is representative of his transcendence. Secondly, if one man does murder another, then the murderer's blood is to be shed *by man* - for man is God's representative, and therefore acts on his behalf in bringing judgment.

It is extremely important to understand the context in which this commandment was originally set. In Genesis 1, God created man in his own image and then told them to "be fruitful and multiply and subdue the earth."

Humanity did become fruitful. By the time of Genesis 6, "men began to increase in number on the earth" (Genesis 6.1). But they were not subduing the earth for God's glory, they were acting as fallen humanity without reference to their Creator. In Genesis 7, God destroyed all of humanity except for Noah's family. In Genesis 8, Noah and his family came out of the ark and began life in a "new creation". Now, please pay close attention.

In Genesis 9, God again repeated his cultural mandate to mankind: "be fruitful and increase in number and fill the earth" (Genesis 9.1). It is in this context that we hear the prohibition to taking human life:

> And for your lifeblood I will surely demand an accounting. I will demand an accounting from every animal. And from each man, too, I will demand an accounting for the life of his fellow man. Whoever sheds the blood of man, by man shall his blood be shed; for in the image of God has God made man (Genesis 9.5,6).

Then, in the same breath, God repeats his mandate to Noah: "As for you, be fruitful and increase in number; multiply on the earth and increase upon it" (Genesis 9.7).

Did you see it? What we have here is a commandment sandwich: two slices of "be fruitful and multiply" with a piece of "don't kill" slipped in between them. Part of man's task on earth is to reproduce, and for the family of humanity to subdue the earth as God's representatives. Murder decreases rather than increases the population expansion that God desires. It actually thwarts God's plan for history.

The Interweaving Of The Covenant

By now you might have noticed that the Ten Commandments are directly related to one another. You can't break only one. If you break one, you have automatically broken others. The sixth commandment begins afresh the covenant outline, but it also relates to the fifth commandment which it follows. The fifth commandment is all about continuity - one generation passing on values and inheritance to another, and honoring those which came before it. The fifth commandment, then, is directly related to the mandate to be fruitful and multiply. The sixth commandment forbids breaking that continuity by murder.

Murder Is Too Strong A Word

The New International Version, which we are using in this book, gives the command as "You shall not murder", but this is not exactly an accurate translation. The Hebrew word (*lo tirtsach*, from the root *ratsach*) means "to kill", and is used in the Old Testament for pretty much any kind of killing, not just murder. What the commandment really says is, "You shall not *kill*" (as most older translations actually read). Some pacifists have taken this to mean that all killing is forbidden, including killing an enemy that invades your country, or killing an intruder that means harm to your family. Where the text gets misunderstood is not in the word "kill", but in the word, "you".

God's command to the people of Israel was "*You* shall not kill" - you, personally; you, singularly; you, of your own decision and volition. As an individual, you do not have the authority to take another human being's life. That life was given to him by God, and only God has the authority to take it away. Period.

God's Hierarchy Doing The Killing Job

Do you remember that we have already learned that God has established three covenantal institutions to enforce his rules - the family, the church, and the state? Each of these hierarchies possesses it's own sanctions, it's own set of blessings and curses. Simply put, the family possesses inheritance and disinheritance; the Church possesses the sacraments, and excommunication; the state, Saint Paul tells us, possesses the power of the sword:

> Everyone must submit himself to the governing authorities, for *there is no authority except that which God has established*. The authorities that exist have been established by God. Consequently, he who rebels against the authority is rebelling against what God has instituted, and those who do so will bring judgment on themselves. For rulers hold no terror for those who do right, but for those who do wrong. Do you want to be free from fear of the one in authority? Then do what is right and he will commend you. For he is God's servant to do you good. But if you do wrong, be afraid, for *he does*

not bear the sword for nothing. He is
God's servant, an agent of wrath to bring
punishment on the wrongdoer" (Romans
13.1-4).

You must remember that Paul is writing
this epistle while the godless and maniacal
Roman Emperors were "the governing
authorities". He is not saying that all
governments, no matter how evil, are doing
God's will. He *is* saying that the very notion of
civil government is God's idea (those
governments have a responsibility to not make
their own rules, but to righteously represent
God, but that is another story).

Paul is also saying that those civil
governments have the sanction of the sword
and *can* use it righteously! What I'm going to
say next may be startling and easily
misunderstood, so approach it carefully.

William T. Cavanaugh, in an
outstanding essay on this commandment,
begins by saying "The Lord God said, 'You
shall not kill,' and yet those who profess to be
bound by these words do a lot of killing." He
goes on to show that people are always
bemoaning the fact that so many lives are
taken "in the name of God". Then he says this:
"In this essay I will argue precisely the

opposite: killing in the name of God is the only type of killing that could be legitimate."[21]

There is a legitimate taking of human life. The civil authorities have that authorization from Scripture, and this is precisely what God told Noah when he said that if a man takes another man's life, then *by man* his life would be taken. I am not here arguing the merits of the death penalty, I am simply saying that the death penalty is a biblically legitimate action when carried out by the state when it acts as a representative of God.

Historic Christianity has also recognized that life may be taken in the act of self defense, when the intention is not to kill a person, but to protect innocent people. Thomas Aquinas wrote, "The act of self-defense can have a double effect: the preservation of one's own life; and the killing

---

[21] Cavanaugh, William T., *Killing in the Name of God*, found in *I Am The Lord Your God, Christian Reflections on the Ten Commandments*, edited by Carl E. Braaten and Christopher R. Seitz, Grand Rapids, MI, Eerdmans, 2005, p. 127.

of the aggressor...the one is intended, the other is not."[22]

Once again, Joy Davidman sums up the matter with precision and insight:

> Make no mistake about it; violence is here to stay. All we can accomplish with a blanket condemnation is to widen the gulf between the wild and the tame humans - between the lawless materialists who kill when they should not and the nice little humanists who can't kill when they should...We do not make a better world by training the fight out of our little boys; we only make a more cowardly one - a world of murderees inviting the murderers."[23]

The Limits of Taking Life

Even the civil government has biblical limits for the taking of life. It is forbidden to take innocent life: "Have nothing to do with a

---

[22] Thomas Aquinas, *Summa Theologiae* II-II, 64.7; quoted in the *Catechism of the Catholic Church*, Liguori Publications, Liguori, MO, 1994, p. 545.

[23] Davidman, p. 80.

false charge and do not put an innocent or honest person to death, for I will not acquit the guilty" (Exodus 23.7). In our own time the civil governments of many countries are directly responsible for the condoning of the taking of the most innocent lives of all - the unborn. Abortion is *the most direct* violation of God's commands to Moses and Noah, for it destroys human continuity and productivity by killing innocent human beings before they even have the chance to breathe air. In the United States alone more than fifty million lives have been sacrificed to the god of convenience. A nation or culture cannot think it will escape the consequences of such actions, consequences which have been worked into the very fabric of creation and will ultimately bring that nation or culture to ruin.

Life Is Precious

Obviously this command keeps us from "taking the law into our own hands". It also teaches us that there are proper authorities to which we must submit in life. But most importantly, it teaches us that every person we will ever meet is precious in the eyes of the Lord and carries the indelible mark of his likeness in their very being. C.S. Lewis said it best:

It is a serious thing to live in a society of possible gods and goddesses, to remember that the dullest and most uninteresting people you can talk to may one day be a creature which, if you saw it now, you would be strongly tempted to worship, or else a horror and a corruption such as you now meet, if at all, only in a nightmare. All day long we are, in some degree, helping each other to one or another of these destinations. It is in the light of these overwhelming possibilities, it is with awe and circumspection proper to them, that we should conduct all our dealings with one another, all friendships, all loves, all play, all politics. There are no ordinary people. You have never talked to a mere mortal...It is immortals whom we joke with, work with, marry, snub, and exploit - immortal horrors or everlasting splendors.[24]

---

[24] Lewis, C.S., *The Weight Of Glory*, New York, MacMillan, 1949, p. 14f.

Chapter Seven

You Shall Not Commit Adultery

"You shall not commit adultery."

If he had just played along, he could have advanced his place of power and had some illicit fun in the process. Instead he rejected the seductions of the married woman, and landed himself in prison. His name was Joseph and you can read the tale of his resistance to Potiphar's wife in Genesis 39. The intriguing thing is that Joseph foreswore adultery four hundred years before the seventh commandment was given, because the principal was already there, from the time of creation.

This particular commandment has a history of humorous misinterpretations. For example, a version of the King James Bible, popularly called *The Adulterer's Bible*, was printed in 1631 (twenty years after the original), and had to be quickly recalled. The problem was the omission of one three letter word: "not". Exodus 20.14 simply read, "Thou shalt commit adultery". The printer was fined 300 English pounds, the books were destroyed, and only eleven copies remain today! J.I. Packer tells of a young Sunday school student defining the word adultery (because it contained the word *adult*) as, "the sin of pretending to be older than you are".[25]

I have been teaching the Ten Commandments to children for thirty years, but one of the funniest incidents occurred when, having taught them all to my four year old grandson, Kenny, and asking him a few days later, "What is the seventh commandment?", he responded, "You shall not admit adultery!"

As funny as these mistakes are, adultery is no laughing matter. In our culture, where it is still (for the moment) considered a crime to murder, steal, and perjure oneself on the

---

[25] Packer, p. 83.

witness stand (commandments six, eight, and nine), breaking the seventh commandment is looked at with a wink, or at worst a shrugging of the shoulders. Not everyone personally knows a murderer, or a thief, or a perjurer. Everyone personally knows an adulterer. It is the sin of our age. But if it is any consolation, we are not the first generation to make a mess of sex. It has been a problem since Genesis.

Just to make sure we all understand, let me say it clearly: "Adultery is copulating with someone else's spouse, or if married with anyone but the spouse."[26]

Adultery And The Covenant

One of the three covenantal institutions established by God is the family. We have already seen that the fifth commandment, to honor your father and mother, relates directly to the family, and so does this, the seventh commandment.

The first point of covenant is *transcendence*, and is tied to the sixth commandment, "You shall not kill". The second point of covenant is *hierarchy*, and it relates to the seventh commandment, "You

---

[26] Jensen, Robert W., in Braaten, p. 175.

shall not commit adultery." The family, consisting of a married man and woman (and their children) was, as the old marriage ceremony declares, *"established by God in creation*, and our Lord Jesus Christ adorned this manner of life by his presence and first miracle at the wedding in Cana of Galilee". The sin of adultery is a direct assault on this God-established and holy union between a woman and a man.

The Jealousy Of God And Man

We have already seen that the second commandment, "Don't bow down to idols" correlates to the second point of covenant, *hierarchy*. And now we see that this seventh commandment forbidding adultery also relates to *hierarchy*. But watch how these two commandments interrelate.

When God gives the second commandment he declares that his people should not worship idols, "for I, the Lord your God, am a jealous God" (Exodus 20.5). His jealousy over his people is akin to marital jealousy. When God speaks of Israel being unfaithful to him and turning to the idols of the land (thus breaking the second commandment), he sometimes describes their unfaithfulness in terms of adultery. An example is from the time of the Judges, when the people threw off their relationship with God and, "would not listen to their judges but *prostituted themselves* to other gods". The King James Version makes it even stronger: they, "*went a whoring* after other gods" (Judges 2.17; for other examples see Judges 8.27-33, Ezekiel 6.9, Hosea 9.1, and the entire chapter of Ezekiel 16 which is so graphic you will likely never hear it read aloud in a church service).

Both the second and the seventh commandments were given in the historical context of the people of Israel having worshipped a golden calf and participated in sexual immorality, only days before receiving the Law (Exodus 32.6). From the very first instance of giving these commands, then, the forbiddance of idolatry and adultery are uniquely related. Both are a terrible abuse by and of the hierarchy that God has established, be it Church or family.

How To Really Tick Off The Creator

Can you imagine God being so upset with you that he would simply say, "That's it. I'm not even going to listen to your prayers anymore. Cry all you want, I won't even notice!"

Heavens to Betsy, that would be a terrible predicament! But that is exactly where Israel found herself during the days of the prophet Malachi. *What could they have done to rile him up so much?* Malachi tells us:

> Another thing you do: You flood the Lord's altar with tears. You weep and wail because he no longer pays attention to your offerings or accepts them with pleasure from your hands. You ask, "Why?" It is because the Lord is acting as the *witness* between you and the wife of your youth, because you have broken faith with her, though she is your partner, the wife of your marriage *covenant.*
>
> Has not the Lord made them one? In flesh and spirit they are his. And why one? Because he was seeking godly offspring. So guard yourself in your spirit, and do not break faith with the wife of your youth.
>
> "I hate divorce," says the Lord God of Israel, "and I hate a man's covering himself with violence as well as with his garment," says the

Lord Almighty. So guard yourself in your spirit, and do not break faith (Malachi 2.13-1).

Whew! God was angry with his people because of how they were approaching marriage! The men of Israel at this time, having taken Jewess brides in their youth, were in their more mature years divorcing these women and taking up with young heathen girls. It was all the rage. Everyone was doing it. But God wasn't going to put up with it anymore. He was coming to the defense of these Hebrew women and putting a stop to it, or else!

Several truths present themselves in this passage.

Marriage Is A Covenant: Marriage is not a business arrangement. It isn't an informal agreement. It isn't a convenience, it is a covenant. This is why the old matrimony ceremony declares that marriage is "not to be entered into lightly or unadvisedly." Marriage is serious business. When a man and a woman give themselves to each other in marriage, they are establishing a binding covenant of unity, and God himself is serving as the witness. As such, he is also the covenant witness to the broken vows.

In biblical and most all ancient covenants, the arrangement was sealed with blood. The first thing Noah did after the ark landed on dry ground was to offer a sacrifice with the spilling of blood, because he was entering into a new covenant with God. With Abraham the covenant was signified by the blood of circumcision. The New Covenant in Christ was established in his own shed blood on the cross. Another indicator that marriage was seen as a covenant is that the Old Testament Law called for proof of the marriage covenant in blood. When a man accused his wife of not being a virgin before their marriage, a blood-stained cloth from the wedding night was presented by the bride's parents as proof that her virginity was guarded, until the covenant was consummated in the marriage bed (cf. Deuteronomy 22.13-17).

God owns the married couple: By coming into the covenant of marriage, the man and woman have bound themselves not only to one another, but to God. In "flesh and spirit," Malachi tells us, "they are his"(v. 15). Saint Paul echoes this when he concludes his thoughts on sexual purity in 1 Corinthians by adding, "Do you not know that your body is a temple of the Holy Spirit, who is in you, whom you have received from God? *You are not your own; you were bought at a price.* Therefore honor God with your body" (1 Corinthians 6.19-20).

God's purpose in covenant marriage is to produce godly offspring: One of the primary themes of the Bible, beginning in Genesis 1, is God's plan for man and woman to come into unity and produce godly descendants. In the beginning, God created humanity to "be fruitful and multiply". When man sinned and fell, God told the serpent that Eve would have a male descendant, a "seed", who would vindicate her by destroying the serpent: "And I will put enmity between you and the woman, and between your offspring [*seed*] and hers; he will crush your head, and you will strike his heel" (Genesis 3.15). This verse is known as the *protoevangelion* - the first gospel, for it is the first text to prophesy the coming of the Messiah (and, for bonus point, it prophesies him as being the "seed" of the woman - but women don't have seeds, they have eggs - here is a subtle reference to the virgin birth which would later be declared by Isaiah).

From that day in the garden until Christ, God kept talking to his people about their seed. He made the promise of blessed seed to Abraham, and to King David, and finally, to the Blessed Virgin Mary. Jesus *is* the seed of the woman, who did indeed crush the head of the serpent. *But there is more!* Jesus, the Bible tells us, is only "the firstborn among many brothers" (Romans 8.29). He is the prototype of the many seeds to come. The Scriptures also promised that Christ himself would see his offspring - not born of the flesh, but of the Spirit: "Yet it was the Lord's will to crush him and cause him to suffer, and though the Lord makes his life a guilt offering, he will see his offspring [*seed*] and prolong his days, and the will of the Lord will prosper in his hands" (Isaiah 53.10).

Jesus Christ, as the Promised Seed, fulfilled the Old Covenant. But Jesus Christ, as the Promised Seed, also instituted the New Covenant through which God will greatly multiply Christ's seed in the Church, until finally the mandate given to Adam and to Noah is satisfied: Be fruitful and multiply and subdue the earth as representatives of its true King and Lord.

These sons and daughters of the kingdom, these seeds of the Seed, come into existence by conversion, but more importantly, and more covenantally, by birth into a family that fulfills God's purpose in marriage, brings forth godly offspring, and raises them in the nurture and admonition of the Lord.

Adultery, it goes without saying, is a devilish strike against marriage, against the family, and against bringing forth godly offspring.

What About Divorce and Remarriage?

Some of you are probably wishing I would at least touch on the subject of divorce, since we have just heard God say, "I hate divorce". While this isn't the subject of the seventh commandment, it does come into the picture, so I will very briefly and carefully and lightfootedly step where angels fear to tread.

Enough sermons have already been preached on God saying, "I hate divorce" to make any divorcee in the pew feel like crawling under it. But turn the question around. Ask most people who have gone through a divorce and they will side with God - they hate it too! Divorce is ugly, nasty, and not the plan. No young starry-eyed couple ever walked down the aisle with the *intention* of getting a divorce a few years down the road. Divorce always involves sin of some kind, and it is a horrible thing to experience. Both divorcees and God agree on this. But I would suggest that God hates divorce for more than reasons of principle. He also hates it because he has himself experienced it. Remember how we saw Israel's idolatry couched in the language of adultery? Remember how Israel kept leaving her true Lover and "whoring after" false pagan gods? The prophet Jeremiah delivered this message from God to Israel: "I gave faithless Israel her certificate of divorce and sent her away because of all her adulteries" (Jeremiah 3.8). God was certainly the innocent party in this mess, but he experienced the pain of divorce nonetheless.

So what about divorce and remarriage? Well, it depends on who you ask. Jesus said that it was permitted in the Old Covenant Law because of the callousness of humanity, but that divorce wasn't God's plan from the get-go: "Moses permitted you to divorce your wives because your hearts were hard. But it was not this way from the beginning." He then said that divorce is unacceptable with one exception: "I tell you that anyone who divorces his wife, *except for marital unfaithfulness*, and marries another woman commits adultery" (Matthew 19.8-9).[27]

---

[27] For a very insightful study on the covenantal principles of remarriage (and an exploration of just what "marital unfaithfulness" means - it is more than just sleeping around), I highly recommend Ray Sutton's *Second Chance*, Fort Worth, Dominion Press, 1988.

The Roman Catholic Church says sometimes divorce is unavoidable, but remarriage is never in the cards. At the other extreme are some Protestant churches that don't have any position on the subject and don't address it at all. The Greek Orthodox Church, calling as witness to their position the likes of Saint Basil the Great, recognizes the sinful tragedy of divorce, but allows remarriage *as a pastoral concession* in light of human weakness and the corrupt world in which we live. But with the Orthodox it is kind of like baseball, three strikes and you're out.

If you want more than this, talk to your priest or pastor, I'm a busy guy!

Note, however, that even if the major Christian churches cannot agree on what, if anything, constitutes valid divorce and remarriage, they all agree on this: You shall not commit adultery.

So don't.

Chapter Eight

You Shall Not Steal

"You shall not steal."

Frank Abagnale Jr. pretended to be a commercial airline pilot, a surgeon, and a lawyer, and made millions of dollars in the process - before he was 19 years old! His story is recounted in the movie *Catch Me If You Can*, starring Leonardo DiCaprio. I love con artist movies. I love trying to figure out what they are up to and how they do it - *Maverick*, *Oceans Eleven*, *The Sting*, and in my book the funniest con movie ever, *Dirty Rotten Scoundrels* with Steve Martin and Michael Caine.

I love con movies, but I would hate to be conned. My dearly departed grandfather was conned out of a sizable chunk of change back in the early 80's, getting caught up in a scheme where he was assured he could get something for nothing.

The truth of the matter is, there is something in fallen human nature - something in every one of us, that has an inclination to be attracted to something for nothing, and so we are all, at some level, tempted to break the eighth commandment, "You shall not steal".

The Manipulation of Possessions

By now you may have read it enough to remember that the third point of covenant is *ethics*, and it asks the question, "What are the rules of the covenant". The third commandment, and this, the eighth commandment, correlate to this third point of covenant, and they both have to do with *manipulation* - attempting to manipulate the rules in order to meet some selfish desire. We may manipulate the covenant by taking the Lord's name in vain, or by taking someone else's property.

A completely unnecessary side note: I know some of you don't give a tinker's dam (look it up, it isn't profane) about word studies, and wish I would just leave off with them. If that's you, just skip this paragraph. I think the word *manipulate* is an amazing word. It comes from the Latin *manipulus*, which is a combination of two words: *mani*, meaning "hand", and *plere*, meaning "to fill". So, manipulate means to "fill the hand", and originally connoted skillfully handling an object - and later came to mean skillfully handling other people. But people who manipulate by theft do indeed get a hand full. Now, back to your regularly scheduled program...

The third commandment forbids the misuse of God's name, particularly in trying to manipulate a situation by invoking that name. The eighth commandment has to do with manipulating people and property. God has promised prosperity, success, and victory to those who keep his Word. This includes, in the long run, material prosperity. But God has also prescribed the means by which prosperity is accomplished - two things: hard work and faithfulness to God's Word. When a person breaks the eighth commandment he is trying to short circuit God's process. He is trying to manipulate wealth and prosperity rather than gain it through godly means.

Protecting Continuity

Do you remember the last point of covenant? *Continuity*. It is also what the fifth commandment is all about. Remember how you learned at the beginning of this book that the Ten Commandments are the covenant model twice over? Well, here is one more bit of information to help you understand the flow of the Commandments. The fifth commandment is about continuity. Commandments six through ten repeat the covenant model, but *they all have to do with protecting continuity*. Killing and adultery can destroy the continuity of a person or family. So can stealing from them.

There is a terrible story in the book of 1 Kings (chapter 21) which tells of a wicked king and queen, Ahab and Jezebel, stealing a vineyard from a commoner named Naboth. At first Ahab offers to buy the vineyard, but Naboth tells him it is not for sale. The reason Naboth gives is, "The Lord forbid that I should give you the *inheritance* of my fathers" (1 Kings 21.3). The vineyard represented familial continuity to Naboth. When Ahab stole the vineyard he destroyed Naboth's family continuity (not to mention the fact that Naboth's murder also destroyed continuity in his family).

Private Ownership

For any communists or radical socialists who may be reading this book (like that's going to happen), it should be pointed out that you can't have a commandment about stealing without the accompanying social idea of private ownership. It is impossible to steal from someone unless someone *owns* something. Otherwise, you are just taking what *isn't* his.

Of course, God is the true owner of all things (Psalm 50.10-12), but he has sovereignly delegated individuals to be stewards over his wealth. What is yours technically is not yours, but it is yours to *manage* (which also means to *hand*le - but to handle properly; the opposite of manipulate. Sorry, there I go again. Where were we...).

If God owns everything, and if he has called us, through covenantal management, to be co-owners with him, then when a thief steals from an individual that thief is acting in rebellion against God.

Jesus told a story about faithfulness to God, using the very subject we are talking about - possessions. Several truths about private property can be discovered by a careful reading of the tale.

Again, it will be like a man going on a journey, who called his servants and entrusted his property to them. To one he gave five talents of money, to another two talents, and to another one talent, each according to his ability. Then he went on his journey. The man who had received the five talents went at once and put his money to work and gained five more. So also, the one with the two talents gained two more. But the man who had received the one talent went off, dug a hole in the ground and hid his master's money.

After a long time the master of those servants returned and settled accounts with them. The man who had received the five talents brought the other five. "Master," he said, "you entrusted me with five talents. See, I have gained five more."

His master replied, "Well done, good and faithful servant! You have been faithful with a few things; I will put you in charge of many things. Come and share your master's happiness!"

The man with the two talents also came. "Master," he said, "you entrusted me with two talents; see, I have gained two more."

His master replied, "Well done, good and faithful servant! You have been faithful with a few things; I will put you in charge of many things. Come and share your master's happiness!"

Then the man who had received the one talent came. "Master," he said, "I knew that you are a hard man, harvesting where you have not sown and gathering where you have not scattered seed. So I was afraid and went out and hid your talent in the ground. See, here is what belongs to you."

His master replied, "You wicked, lazy servant! So you knew that I harvest where I have not sown and gather where I have not scattered seed? Well then, you should have put my money on deposit with the bankers, so that when I returned I would have received it back with interest.

"Take the talent from him and give it to the one who has the ten talents. For everyone who has will be given more, and he will have an abundance. Whoever does not have, even what he has will be taken from him. And throw that worthless servant outside, into the darkness, where there will be weeping and gnashing of teeth." (Matthew 25.14-31).

While this parable is primarily about how we use the *grace* God has given us, there are three things we should note about private property.

Private property is limited: God has not given wealth to an individual for all eternity, only for his lifetime. I have been blessed to inherit from my father, before his death (long may he live), land on which to build a home. Hopefully, when my wife and I are lying in the grave (having lived to the ripe old age of 155), it will be passed on to our children, and their children after them. They can live on it, or sell it, or whatever they want to do, but it is not theirs forever either. You can't "take it with you" when you die. You are given management of God's wealth to use for *his glory* until your death and his return.

Private property is delegated: All wealth is God's wealth. You have simply been delegated the task of overseeing God's resources. It is your responsibility to refine and multiply what God has given you, and to prove yourself a good steward of what he has entrusted to you.

Private property is covenantal: God gives people wealth in the hope that they will be faithful to him, and he will take wealth away from them if they are not faithful to him. While this may not be obvious in an individual's lifetime, over a period of three or four generations it becomes evident (cf. Exodus 20.5). Those who are faithful to God are the truly prosperous ones in the long run, while the wicked person's wealth is stored up for the righteous (Proverbs 13.22).

In regard to private ownership, we must also establish that the state does not have the God-ordained authority to steal from the people. This is one of the lessons taught in the story of Ahab and Naboth. Theft is theft, even by majority vote. The abuse of general taxes, property taxes, inheritance taxes, and eminent domain is an attempt of the government to usurp the continuity of the family. A welfare state seeks to replace God with itself, causing the people to look to *it* for salvation instead of to God. As a kind of false god, it also attempts to control and override the other two hierarchies established by God - the family and the Church. I can't help it if I leak libertarianism here. God has called the civil government to serve the people and not vice versa.

Stealing From God

This next section is guaranteed to step on the toes of most church-going Christians. We have already seen that *any* theft is theft from God, because everything belongs to him. But, what about theft that is blatant and direct and perpetrated by God's own children? In the book of Malachi, God told Israel that their adulteries were shutting his ears (see Chapter Seven). Then he tells them that their stealing from him was plugging up the heavenly spout where the blessings come out. God says to his people,

> "Will a man rob God? Yet you rob me. But you ask, 'How do we rob you?' *In tithes and offerings*. You are

under a curse - the whole nation of you - because you are robbing me. Bring the whole tithe into the storehouse, that there may be food in my house. Test me in this," says the Lord Almighty, "and see if I will not throw open the floodgates of heaven and pour out so much blessing that you will not have room enough for it. I will prevent pests from devouring your crops, and the vines in your fields will not cast their fruit," says the Lord Almighty. "Then all the nations will call you blessed, for yours will be a delightful land," says the Lord Almighty (Malachi 3.8-12).

Because Israel was unfaithful in the principle of the tithe, they were robbing God, and were under a *covenantal curse* (remember sanctions?). "But," you may say, "That was the Old Covenant, and we are under the New Covenant of grace!" Laying aside for a moment that every commandment we are studying in this book is from the Old Covenant (and are all called *good* in the New Covenant), I would suggest to you that tithing is *not* an Old Covenant principle!

Abraham lived five hundred years before the giving of the Law at Sinai, yet he tithed. After victory in a fierce battle, Abraham was blessed by the great priest Melchizedek:

> Then Melchizedek king of Salem brought out bread and wine. He was priest of God Most High, and he blessed Abram, saying, "Blessed be Abram by God Most High, Creator of heaven and earth. And blessed be God Most High, who delivered your enemies into your hand." *Then Abram gave him a tenth of everything* (Genesis 14.18-20).

Now put two and two together. First, in the New Testament we are told that Jesus is a *"priest forever* in the order of Melchizedek" (Hebrews 5.6,10, 6.20, 7.11-17). This means that the priestly line of Jesus (including the Apostles, those they ordained, and those who serve in his ministry right on down through history to this very moment) are in the line of Melchizedek. So far, so good?

Here is the second thing. The New Testament also declares that all those who have faith in Christ are children of Abraham: "If you belong to Christ, then you are

Abraham's seed, and heirs according to the promise" (Galatians 3.29).

Abraham, our father, who lived by faith, tithed to Melchizedek five hundred years before the Law was given. We, who are Abraham's seed, are called to tithe to Jesus, and his ordained ministers, two thousand years after the Law was fulfilled in Christ.

How many Christians would never think to steal from their neighbors, yet don't think twice about stealing from God?

"But I just can't tithe," some say. "I really want to, and someday I will, but I can't right now." As a pastor who has been in the same church for seventeen years, I know people who have been saying this for seventeen years. And they don't give any more now than they did at the start. Oddly, they can afford new automobiles and nice vacations and pools in their backyards, but they can't afford to give to God. Let me be so bold as to rephrase what they are saying: "I just can't stop stealing from God. I really want to, and someday I will, but I can't right now".

Everything you have belongs to God, and is therefore *holy*. All he asks is that you give a tithe - one tenth - back to him. That tenth is laid on his altar, and the rest - which is also holy - is released for *common* use (pizza, electric bills, gasoline, car payments, insurance, etc.). But if the tenth is not given, the 90% is not released, and the non-tither is therefore using what is holy for common use, an abuse that has negative consequences attached to it.

God told the High Priest Aaron, "You must distinguish between the *holy* and the *common*" (Leviticus 10.10). Later, the prophet Ezekiel condemned the sons of Aaron for forgetting this: "Her priests do violence to my law and profane my holy things; *they do not distinguish between the holy and the common; they teach that there is no difference between the unclean and the clean*; and they shut their eyes to the keeping of my Sabbaths, so that I am profaned among them" (Ezekiel 22.2). Sadly, many if not most Christians have forgotten how to do this because they hold little or nothing as holy in life.

Allow me to challenge you with the same challenge God gave Israel in the book of Malachi: "'Bring the whole tithe into the storehouse, that there may be food in my house. Test me in this,' says the Lord Almighty, 'and see if I will not throw open the floodgates of heaven and pour out so much blessing that you will not have room enough for it'" (Malachi 3. 10).

How To Stop Stealing

The church in Ephesus had folk in it who used to be thieves, and apparently still were. Paul wrote to them, "He who has been stealing must steal no longer, but must work, doing something useful with his own hands, that he may have something to share with those in need" (Ephesians 4.28). This verse tells us two things about thieves - they will not work and they will not give (instead, they take). To turn from thievery, Paul says, involves three things.

Honesty: The one who has been stealing must "steal no longer". He must abandon his *manipulative lifestyle* and become honest in his dealings.

Work: The one who has been stealing must "work, doing something useful with his own hands". Honest work is one of the God-ordained means of prosperity and victory. Labor produces goods, which produce wealth.

Charity: The one who has been stealing must change from taking what *is not* his and start giving what *is* his. he must "share with those in need".

The truly Christian model of life, in contrast to the thief, is one who goes above and beyond the technicality of the tithe and joyfully gives of his own resources; one who gives, "not reluctantly or under compulsion, for God loves a cheerful giver" (2 Corinthians 9.7).

I double dog dare you to cultivate a habit of tithing and generosity, and see what the Lord will do with your faithfulness!

Chapter Nine

You Shall Not Bear False Witness

"You shall not give false testimony against your neighbor."

The married couple had promised to make a significant contribution to the church, to help care for an unexpected influx of travelers who had never heard the gospel, had converted to Christ, and needed some training before they went home. They said they would sell some land and donate the money to the cause. At the last minute, they thought perhaps they would keep *some* of the money from the sale for themselves. Fair enough.

Nothing wrong with that. But what happened next was terrible. The husband brought the money to the pastor and said, "Here is every penny from the land sale - use it well!" And then he dropped dead on the spot. But not before the pastor said, "You are such a liar! You didn't have to give everything you made, but you should have been truthful about it! You have lied to God!" Bang. Dead. On the floor. His wife came in and fell down dead too. Tough consequences for sure, but biblical consequences.

Just in case you think the story is made up, I will give you the reference: The book of Acts, chapter five. The couple's names were Ananias and Sapphira, and the pastor was the Apostle Peter.

God *Hates* Lying

"Whew," you might say, "I'm glad *I* don't lie to God!" But on some level, every lie is a lie to God. Lies, especially by those who bear his name, are an affront to the very nature of God, "who does not lie" (Titus 1.2) and "who does not change like the shifting shadows" (James 1.17).

You see, there isn't a single false bone in God's body. It is impossible for him to lie. It is completely contrary to his very nature. It is Satan who is "a liar and the father of lies" (John 8.44). So just whose character do we portray when we lie? God can't endure the stuff. Solomon in his wisdom wrote,

> There are six things the Lord hates,
> seven that are detestable to him:
> haughty eyes,
> *a lying tongue,*
> hands that shed innocent blood,
> a heart that devises wicked schemes,
> feet that are quick to rush into evil,
> *a false witness who pours out lies*
> and a man who stirs up dissension
> among brothers (Proverbs 6.16-19).

Twice in his list of seven things lying is mentioned! Liars, the Bible tells us, can't even come into the presence of God!

> Lord, who may dwell in your
> sanctuary? Who may live on your
> holy hill?

> He whose walk is blameless and
> who does what is righteous,
> who *speaks the truth from his heart*
> and has *no slander on his tongue,*
> who *does his neighbor no wrong*
> and *casts no slur on his fellowman,*

who despises a vile man but honors
those who fear the Lord,
who keeps his oath even when it
hurts,
who lends his money without usury
and does not accept a bribe against
the innocent.

He who does these things
will never be shaken (Psalm 15).

The powerful prayer prayed at the beginning of most Anglican services (written by Thomas Cranmer) declares, "Almighty God, unto whom all hearts are open, all desires known, and from whom no secrets are hidden..." Cranmer was just echoing the writer of Hebrews:

For the word of God is living and active. Sharper than any double-edged sword, it penetrates even to dividing soul and spirit, joints and marrow; it judges the thoughts and attitudes of the heart. Nothing in all creation is hidden from God's sight. Everything is uncovered and laid bare before the eyes of him to whom we must give account" (Hebrews 4.12-13).

You can't pull the wool over God's eyes.

Lying And The Covenant

The ninth commandment, as it is stated in scripture, is not specifically a prohibition to lying. It is a prohibition to "bearing false witness against your neighbor". In other words, it is a court-related commandment which declares, as it correlates to the fourth point of covenant, that we should not try to monkey with the blessings and curses, the *sanctions*, delivered in justice.

A lying witness gives false testimony, seeking to change the outcome of a trial. There are two ways of doing this.

Let's say you have a nemesis who is on trial for a particular offense. This gal hates you, and you wouldn't mind at all seeing her sent up the river for a few years. So you testify, "I saw her do it," when you know good and well that she was someplace else that night and *did not* do it.

The opposite scenario is that you have a good friend - a close buddy, and he has been accused of a crime which you know good and well he *did* commit, but you go to the stand and say, "He couldn't have done it, he was with me the whole time." It reminds me of the lyrics of one of my favorite Bob Dylan songs. In the story, the singer has committed a crime and is on trial. But his girlfriend comes to his aid:

> Well, you saw my picture in the Corpus Christi Tribune.
>
> Underneath it, it said, "A man with no alibi."
>
> You went out on a limb to testify for me, you said I was with you.
>
> Then when I saw you break down in front of the judge and cry real tears,
>
> It was the best acting I saw anybody do.[28]

Breaking the ninth commandment, of course, isn't done just in courtrooms. It happens all the time when, like Dylan's lady, people do their "acting" to persuade others to believe a falsehood about someone else. Ray Sutton wrote, "Bearing false witness interferes with and perverts judgment...[it] causes

---

[28] Bob Dylan, *Brownsville Girl*, from the album *Knocked Out Loaded*, Copyright ©1986 Special Rider Music.

blessings to fall on those who deserve a curse, and vice versa."[29]

The Power Of The Tongue

We live in a political world, and the *lingua franca* of politics is lying. But politicians lie because it works, and with their falsehoods they are able to sway whole nations into believing and following them. This is because the tongue, though it is small, is the most powerful part of the human body. James, the brother of Jesus, wrote to the clergy under his care and told them,

> When we put bits into the mouths of horses to make them obey us, we can turn the whole animal. Or take ships as an example. Although they are so large and are driven by strong winds, they are steered by a very small rudder wherever the pilot wants to go. Likewise the tongue is a small part of the body, but it makes great boasts. Consider what a great forest is set on fire by a small spark. The tongue also is a fire, a world of evil among the parts of the body. It corrupts the whole person, sets the

[29] Sutton, p. 222.

whole course of his life on fire, and is itself set on fire by hell.

All kinds of animals, birds, reptiles and creatures of the sea are being tamed and have been tamed by man, but no man can tame the tongue. It is a restless evil, full of deadly poison. (James 3.3-8).

Wars have been fought, marriages have been destroyed, friendships have ended, and innocent people have died because of the terrible power of a false tongue.

But in the end, lying usually gets found out. Remember the simple verse by Sir Walter Scott taught to children in past generations?

Oh what a tangled web we weave, When first we practice to deceive!

What begins as a seemingly harmless lie ends up having other lies added to it and then things get really complicated. I love the story of the lying butcher. A customer came in to buy a chicken, so the butcher drew the only chicken he had left out of the ice-packed barrel and said, "Five pounds." When the customer said she wanted a bigger one, the butcher put the chicken back into the barrel, and pulled up the same chicken again. He put it on the scales, pressed a little extra with his thumb, and announced, "Seven pounds". To which the customer replied, "That's perfect! I think I'll take both of them!"

As the Germans say, "'*Lügen haben kurze Beine*' - 'Lies have short legs'. That means lies will always eventually be outrun by the truth."[30]

I admire Winston Churchill, but he was not one to always act in the most Christian way. Speaking once about the need for deceit in times of enemy attack, he said, "In wartime, truth is so precious that she should always be attended by a bodyguard of lies." The telling thing about this line is that Joseph Stalin loved it! While, in espionage, there may be merit to what he said, let me tell you something else that is surrounded by a bodyguard of lies: other sins. Adam ate the forbidden fruit and lied about it. Cain killed his brother and lied about it. Joseph's brothers sold him into slavery and lied about it. Ananias stole from God and lied about it. Chances are you have used lies as a bodyguard too. Speaking falsehood is a vicious, destructive and very powerful tool.

---

[30] Hütter, Reinhard, in Braaten, p. 196.

What's In A Name?

In biblical cultures (and in modern western culture until recently), there was a great significance placed on a person's name. To begin with, there was a great significance placed on *God's* name (see the third commandment). A person's name means a person's character. To misuse God's name is to misrepresent God's character. In the same way, to lie about someone, especially in court, is to give that person an undeserved bad name. To bear false witness against someone is to *steal* that person's character. This commandment is given to guard a man's or a woman's name - his or her character - from slander.

Obviously, the greatest name we can besmirch by our lying is the name of Jesus Christ. We are called "Christians" - followers of Christ. In our baptism we have taken his name as our own. We are members of his body and represent his Church with our every word and action. The reason Saint Paul gives for not lying is this: "Therefore each of you must put off falsehood and speak truthfully to his neighbor, *for we are all members of one body*" (Ephesians 4.25). When we lie or bear false witness about our neighbor, we not only harm others, we harm ourselves - we harm the body of Christ of which we are part.

May I Lie To Save My Baby?

First, I knew you were going to ask that. Anytime this commandment is thoroughly addressed, the question of "ethical lying" comes up: "Is lying ever the right thing to do?" The short answer is, "Yes." I must warn you, what comes next is like playing with dynamite.

Let me rephrase the question: "Does the God require us to tell the truth at all times?" While the Bible forbids us to bear false witness and to lie, it does not demand that we speak the full truth to those who have no business knowing it. Solomon said, "A gossip betrays a confidence, but a trustworthy man keeps a secret" (Proverbs 11.13). R.J. Rushdoony, in his monumental work on the Ten Commandments, wrote,

> The commandment is very clear: we are not to bear false witness against our neighbor, but this does not mean that our neighbor or our enemy is ever entitled to the truth from us, or any word from us, about matters of no concern to them, or of private

nature to us. No enemy or criminal has any right to knowledge from us which can be used to do us evil. Scripture does not condemn Abraham and Isaac for lying in order to avoid murder and rape (Genesis 12.11-13, 20.2, 26.6-7); on the contrary, both are richly blessed by God, and the men who placed them in such an unhappy position are condemned or judged (Genesis 12.15-20, 20.3-18, 26.10-16). Likewise examples abound in Scripture. No one who seeks to do us evil, to violate the law in reference to us or to another, is entitled to the truth.[31]

Other examples of people who either did not tell the full truth or lied to God's enemies are the Hebrew midwives (Exodus 1.15-21), the prostitute Rahab (Joshua 2.1-24), and the prophet Samuel (1 Samuel 16.1-3). In all these instances, God blessed these people for fearing and honoring God above men.

---

[31] Rushdoony, R.J., *The Institutes Of Biblical Law*, Phillipsburg, NJ, The Presbyterian And Reformed Publishing Company, 1973, p. 543).

The point of this is not to create some loophole for all liars, but to show that honoring God is our number one priority in life. The Law was not given as a taskmaster, but as a tool for righteous victory. We must live by the spirit of the Law which seeks, above all, to strengthen and bless God's people and to bring glory to him. Clearly, there is no biblical suggestion that by brutal honesty we should destroy innocent lives and abuse God's Word.

J.I. Packer asks, in response to this line of thinking, "But does that square with the ninth commandment?" Then he answers himself,

> What is forbidden is false witness against your neighbor - that is, as we have said, prideful lying designed to do him down and exalt you at his expense. The positive command implicit in this negative is that we should seek our neighbor's good and speak truth to him and about him to this end. When the love that seeks this good prompts us to withhold truth that, if spoken, would bring him harm, the spirit of the ninth commandment is being observed. In such exceptional cases...all courses

of action have something of evil in
them, and an outright lie, like that of
Rahab, may actually be the best
way, the least evil, and the truest
expression of love to all the parties
involved."[32]

The Opposite Of Lying

If we are not to bear false witness,
then what are we to do? We are to bear
true witness. Jesus, the Bible declares, is
"the faithful witness" (Revelation 1.5). In
the book of Acts, moments before he
ascended to Glory, Jesus told his
disciples to return to Jerusalem and wait
for the promised Holy Spirit: "But you
will receive power when the Holy Spirit
comes on you; and you will *be my witnesses*
in Jerusalem, and in all Judea and
Samaria, and to the ends of the
earth" (Acts 1.8). Just as Jesus is the
faithful witness, we too are called to be
faithful witnesses, speaking the truth of
his goodness and mercy to our neighbor,
and to the many who are far off.

We should not simply avoid the
false, we should embrace the true. Luther

---

[32] Packer, p. 98.

summed up this commandment by writing, "We should fear and love God that we may not deceitfully belie, betray, slander, nor defame our neighbor, but defend him, speak well of him, and put the best construction on everything."[33]

In other words, not only with our actions, but with our *words*, we should be Christ to those around us.

---

[33] Luther, Martin, *Small Catechism*, St. Louis, Concordia Press, 1943 , p. 75.

The Tenth Commandment

You Shall Not Covet

"You shall not covet your neighbor's house. You shall not covet your neighbor's wife, or his manservant or maidservant, his ox or donkey, or anything that belongs to your neighbor."

There she was, soaking in a rooftop hot tub, in all her naked splendor. This was not, mind you, some kind of seductive exhibitionism - she was a married woman faithful to her husband, and she was relaxing in the warm water, bathing in the cool glow of the moonlight. Where no one could see her. Yet someone did see her. Someone from above was looking down on her, and I don't mean God.

She was married to a high ranking lieutenant, and lived in the nicest part of the city, an upscale community just next to the king's palace, and the king, who couldn't sleep that night, went out for a walk along the parapets, when the shimmer of the moonlight on her bathing body caught his eye. She was the most beautiful creature he had ever seen, and he had seen his share of beautiful creatures. Who is this portrait of heaven, he asked himself, and he couldn't erase from his mind what he had seen, and he didn't even try.

The next morning he sent his servants to discover her name, and discovered instead that she was married to one of his most faithful officers. Still, what beat within his chest for her was so strong, he invited her to the palace, and she slept with him. It was a one time encounter, but once was enough to change everything. A month later she sent a message to the king - "I am pregnant".

As men of political power are wont to do, he set out to cover up his compromise. He called the lieutenant in from the fields, commanding him to take a much needed time of rest and relaxation, hoping he would sleep in his own bed, with his own wife, and that the child to be born could be passed off as the husband's, not the philanderer's. But the honorable soldier refused to stay in the luxury of his own home while his men were out standing against the enemy. So the king had his faithful comrade sent to the front line, and ordered his general to expose him to the fiercest place of the battle, and to withdraw troops at just the right moment, to assure the death of the angel's husband. There he died, in the field of battle, defending the king who stole his wife, and his life.

In one swift movement, King David had broken the first, second, fifth, sixth, seventh, eight and ninth commandment. But it all started with his breaking the tenth: You shall not covet. You can read the whole story in 2 Samuel 11.

Break The Law A Little And You Break The Law A Lot

It can be said that the person who truly obeys the first commandment with all his heart automatically keeps the rest of the commandments. Likewise, when a person breaks the tenth commandment it lays the groundwork for breaking the rest. When James, as the bishop of Jerusalem, wrote to the priests under his care, he corrected them for the covetousness in their hearts that led to all kinds of other sins:

> What causes fights and quarrels among you? Don't they come from your desires that battle within you? You want something but don't get it. You kill and covet, but you cannot have what you want. You quarrel and fight. You do not have, because you do not ask God. When you ask, you do not receive, because you ask with wrong motives, that you may spend what you get on your pleasures (James 4.1-3).

And you thought clergy today were a mess! These men were called to shepherd the people of God, but instead found themselves in bitter disarray because the attitude of their hearts led to all kinds of ungodly behavior (it is a worthwhile exercise to take an hour and read the whole book of James - it is only five chapters - and apply it to church leadership instead of the general Christian people; it also serves as a remarkable commentary on keeping the Ten Commandments).

John Chrysostom, the fourth century bishop of Constantinople, echoed James in his sermon on 2 Corinthians 27, when he described the covetousness of Christians in his own day:

> We fight one another, and envy arms us against one another...If everyone strives to unsettle the Body of Christ, where shall we end up? We are engaging in making Christ's Body a corpse...We declare ourselves members of one and the same organism, yet we devour one another like beasts."[34]

Saint James wrote, "For whoever keeps the whole law and yet stumbles at just one point is guilty of breaking all of it" (James 2.10). The Law is not a checklist of ten items, some of which you are guilty of breaking and some of which you are not. It is an integrated whole, and to transgress in one part is to transgress it all. This is nowhere more true than in the tenth commandment.

Coveting And The Covenant

"You shall not covet" corresponds to the fifth point of covenant, *continuity*. The book of

---

[34] John Chrysostom, *Homily on 2 Corinthians 27.3-4*, cited in the *Catechism of the Catholic Church*, p. 607.

Exodus lists seven things you are forbidden to covet -

> your neighbor's house,
> your neighbor's wife,
> his manservant,
> his maidservant,
> his ox,
> his donkey,
> anything that belongs to your neighbor.

It isn't as if these are the only things we are forbidden to covet. Seven is "the perfect number" and represents the perfection and completeness of a person's life. Notice, that the list represents all the ingredients of a person's or a family's *continuity*: the home where life is lived, the spouse through whom children are born, the servants (employees) and tools through which a person makes a living and gets ahead in life. This commandment forbids coveting *anything* which God has given to another, and which is rightfully his.

I Want It So Bad

Coveting is another way of saying lusting. We tend to isolate lust to one area - the sexual - but lust (the old word for it is *concupiscence*) means to inordinately desire. It is "the movement of the sensitive appetite contrary to the operation of human reason."[35] Shakespeare defined it, "Past reason hunted, and no sooner had, past reason hated."[36]

This final commandment leans in the direction of what Jesus will say centuries later, when he teaches that murder and adultery are not just physical acts, but that the man who hates his brother or lusts after a woman has already committed murder and adultery in his heart (Matthew 5.21-30). While the first nine commandments are broken by *action*, the tenth commandment is broken by *thought*.

To covet is to desire persons, or relationships, or goods which you have neither earned nor inherited, nor are willing to acquire by godly means. Some "covet words" are jealousy, envy and resentment. In coveting, a person will become jealous over another's achievements or possessions, and even resent that others have acquired success. Sometimes this attitude leads to not only desiring another's blessings, but even desiring that the other person would meet with failure - "if I can't have it, then neither should he". Perhaps

---

[35] *Catechism Of The Catholic Church*, p. 602.

[36] William Shakespeare, Sonnet 129.

you remember the old Aesop's fable which tells of a man freeing a genie who grants him any wish he commands, with one condition: his arch enemy will receive double. After much anguish the man finally decided what to ask for. He approached the genie and said, "I wish to be blind in one eye."

Ideas Have Consequences

While the sin of coveting is a sin of attitude and thought, it leads to action. The Hebrew word for covenant (*chamad*) speaks, not only of wicked desires, but also of taking the thing which is desired (if given the opportunity).

In the book of Joshua there is a story of a selfish man named Achan whose lustful sin caused the defeat of Israel in a battle, and eventually the death of himself and his family. He came upon a hoard of enemy treasure, which God had commanded to be destroyed. Instead, Achan "*coveted* them and *took* them" (Joshua 7.21). The prophet Micah spoke of the wicked men of Israel and Judah who, "*covet* fields and *seize them*, and houses, and *take them*. They *defraud* a man of his home, a fellowman of his inheritance" (Micah 2.2.).

Sin is conceived in the heart, in the attitude and motives of a person, and is birthed in the action. Saint James describes the process perfectly: "but each one is tempted when, by his own evil desire, he is dragged away and enticed. Then, after desire has conceived, it gives birth to sin; and sin, when it is full-grown, gives birth to death" (James 1.14-15).

Notice the process. The sin is first conceived in the interior of a person's being - in the heart. Long before the action occurs, the sin already exists - it is conceived - it is alive. It is given birth when the idea is acted upon, but it is already alive and growing in the womb of the thought-life. After it is born - after it becomes an action - it gives birth to death. The end consequence of sin is always some kind of death.

Coveting Is Idolatry

To covet another person's possessions or relationships is to place one's desire for those things above one's desire for God, making these things gods and idols. Saint Paul wrote, "For of this you can be sure: No immoral, impure or *greedy* [*covetous*] person - *such a man is an idolater* - has any inheritance in the kingdom of Christ and of God" (Ephesians

5.5), and, "Put to death, therefore, whatever belongs to your earthly nature: sexual immorality, impurity, lust, evil desires and *greed* [*covetousness*], *which is idolatry*" (Colossians 3.5).

To break the tenth commandment is to automatically break the first and second, even when there is not action taken, for in coveting we are placing other things before our relationship with God.

The Antidote For Covetousness

The sin of coveting is more subtle than the other infractions of the Ten Commandments. It permeates the modern society. The economic systems of capitalism and socialism and communism are all alike afflicted with it. It infiltrates our social relationships ("keeping up with the Joneses"); it is prevalent in our churches. Because it is a heart attitude more than an action, it is harder to identify and deal with. It sneaks up on you and takes root before you know it. Nevertheless, here is an antidote to covetousness: "Seek first his kingdom and his righteousness, and all these things will be given to you as well" (Matthew 6.33). Our priority must be the kingdom of God. When we - as individuals, as churches, as families, as societies, as nations - become kingdom seekers, all other desires fall into their appropriate place (which, for many desires, is the garbage can). When we seek first the righteousness, peace, and joy given through the Holy Spirit (for this *is* the definition of the kingdom of God - Romans 14.17), selfish ambition falls by the wayside.

In writing to Timothy, Paul said, "godliness with contentment is great gain" (1 Timothy 6.6). We must learn to be content with the calling God has given us (1 Corinthians 7.1, Philippians 4.11, Hebrews 13.5). This is not an admonition to have no vision, no dream, no goals - without these a people perish (Proverbs 29.18). It is an admonition, however, to simultaneously cling to a vision for tomorrow, and work toward it, while being content today in the place God has positioned us.

Instead of coveting what rightfully belongs to others, the Bible tells us to, "*earnestly desire* [*covet* - KJV] the greater gifts" (1 Corinthians12.31). So, there is such a thing as godly coveting after all - when we press forward to the mark of our high calling.

In teaching children this commandment, I have used the simplified and age-old line, "Put God first, others second, and me last." This is really what it means to not covet. J.I. Packer agrees:

> When people shy away from the formula "God first, others second, self last," as if it were a recipe for total misery, they show that they do not understand themselves. Actually, this is the only formula that has ever brought true inward freedom and contentment on a lifelong basis to anyone.[37]

And so the Ten Commandments end where they began. They are a circle after all. To keep the tenth commandment, just keep the first one. In fact, to truly keep the first is to keep them all. As Saint Augustine said, "Love God, and do as you please".

---

[37] Packer, p. 111.

Postscript

There Is No Condemnaton

Psalm 119, the longest chapter in the whole Bible, is King David's litany of praise for the beauty of the Law. Yes, King David, the man who so violated the Law in his life, also loved it. The Bible tells us that, in spite of his terrible sins and failures, God called David, "a man after my own heart" (Acts 13.22).

Writing this book has been an exercise of conviction for me, as I hope reading it has been for you. How can a sinner like me write of keeping God's righteous commandments? And yet, I would remind you, it is conviction that should come here, not condemnation, for Saint Paul tells us, "there is now no condemnation for those who are in Christ Jesus" (Romans 8.1).

To study the Law of God is to study our own shortcomings and failures. On every page we see where we have not loved God with all our hearts and have not loved our neighbors as ourselves. But this is precisely one of the purposes of the Law in the first place - to show us that we cannot measure up in our own selves, and that we need the grace and mercy of God that comes through Christ. He is the one who has kept the law, and has exchanged our own sins for his righteousness. Saint Paul continues,

> because through Christ Jesus the law of the Spirit of life set me free from the law of sin and death. For what the law was powerless to do in that it was weakened by the sinful nature, God did by sending his own Son in the likeness of sinful man to be a sin offering. And so he condemned sin in sinful man, in order that the righteous requirements of the law might be fully met *in us*, who do not live according to the sinful nature but according to the Spirit (Romans 8.2-4).

My prayer, for myself and for you, is that we will not look upon this Law of God as an oppressive yoke to keep us from freedom, for this it is not, but that we would, rather, join with that old sinner King David, and see these commandments as beautiful instruments to bring us prosperity, and joy, and long life:

I will walk about in freedom,
for I have sought out your precepts...
...for I delight in your commands
because I love them.
-Psalm 119.45-47

Appendix One

Teaching The Commandments
To Children

In 1986 I wrote a one year curriculum on covenant for the Sunday School program at Living Word Chapel in Forest, Wisconsin. It was geared to be used by teachers for all ages from preschool to adult. It was never published, but became a source I have returned to time and again, including for much of the content of this book.

The section on the Ten Commandments in the curriculum included coloring sheets meant to help the children memorize the Commandments. It was something I had to create for a Betty Botz's Child Evangelism class in Bible College. I have discovered, over the years, that the sheets not only help children memorize them and be able to name them off in any order asked, but they also assist adults in remembering them. I promise you, if you make your own set, you will never forget them.

While working on the curriculum, I gave my original posters to my friend, Peter E. Newcombe, who crafted the coloring sheets for me. I have long since lost contact with Peter. So, Peter, if you see this, please get in touch!

On the following pages are the Ten Commandment coloring sheets created by Peter and me. On the back of each page is a short hint for teaching the children. If you would like a PDF set of these, formatted to 8.5x11, they can be downloaded at www.kennethmyers.net.

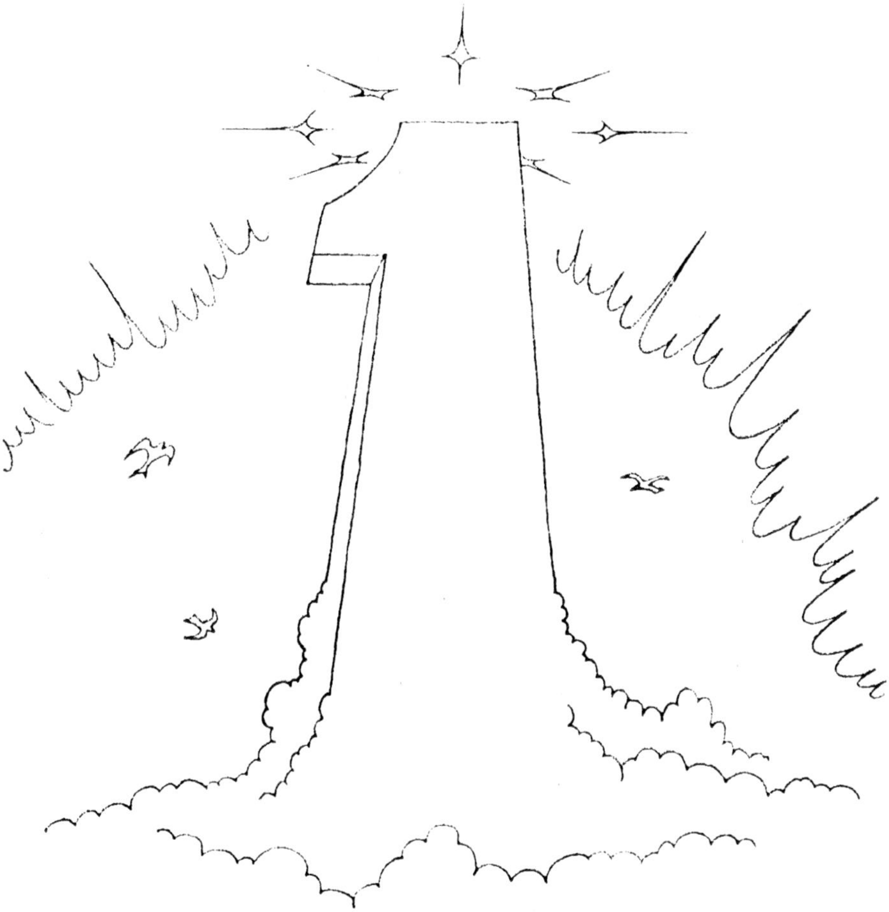

The First Commandment

You Shall Have
No Other Gods Before Me
or
"Put God First"

"Put God first" is an easy way for children to say this commandment.

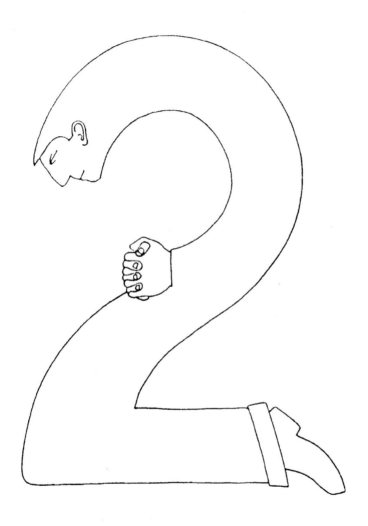

The Second Commandment

You Shall Not Bow Dow To Idols

This picture shows someone in the shape of a 2 bowing down and worshipping. The only one we are to worship is God. Don't bow down to idols.

The Third Commandment

You Shall Not Misuse God's Name

Here are two people misusing God's name. The first (on the top half of the three) is using God's name jokingly, the second (on the bottom half) is using God's name in anger. God's name is special, and we should not misuse it in silliness or anger.

This picture (and the seventh) might be a little difficult to remember, and should be practiced more than the others.

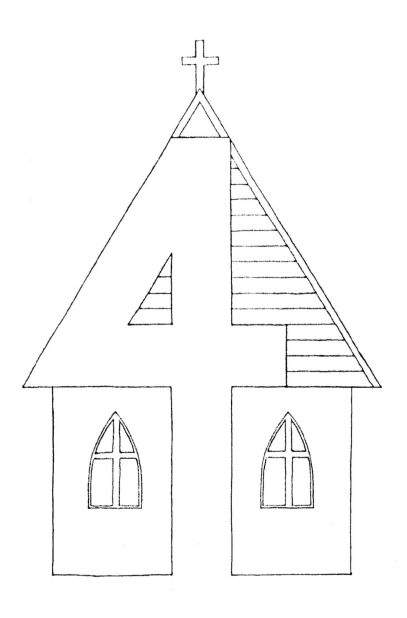

The Fourth Commandment

Remember The Sabbath
or
"Go To Church"

The easiest way to help children understand the Sabbath is by instilling in them the honor of God in worshipping on the Lord's Day. Go to church.

221

The Fifth Commandment

Honor Your Father And Your Mother
or
"Treat Your Dad And Mom
Like Kings And Queens"

This picture, with the crown, is easy to tie to the fifth commandment, but because the shape of 5 has nothing to do with the crown, it might be a little difficult to remember. Over time, repetition will firmly seal it in the mind.

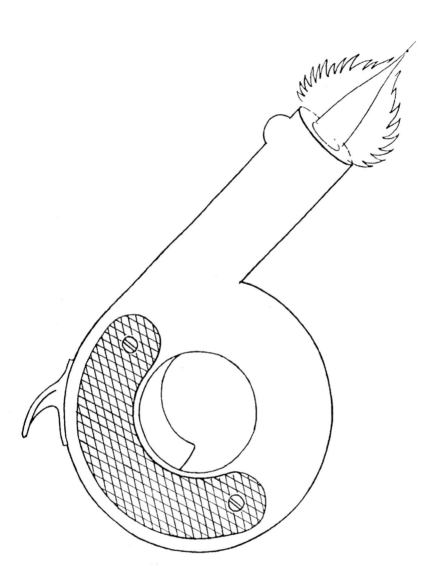

The Sixth Commandment

You Shall Not Kill

Sometimes, people kill other people with guns. This little pistol reminds us that we should not kill people, because all people are special in God's eyes.

The Seventh Commandment

You Shall Not Commit Adultery

How do you explain adultery to a child? Perhaps the easiest way is by saying that God intends men and women to be married to and to love just one spouse. For someone to try and steal another person's spouse is adultery.

This picture is the number 7 set in the figure of a man's face. The man is Joseph. Tell the story of how Potiphar's wife tried to get Joseph to be her lover instead of her own husband, but Joseph refused. If you make he seven multi-colored, it can also remind the children of the story of Joseph's coat of many colors, helping them associate the picture with his name and story.

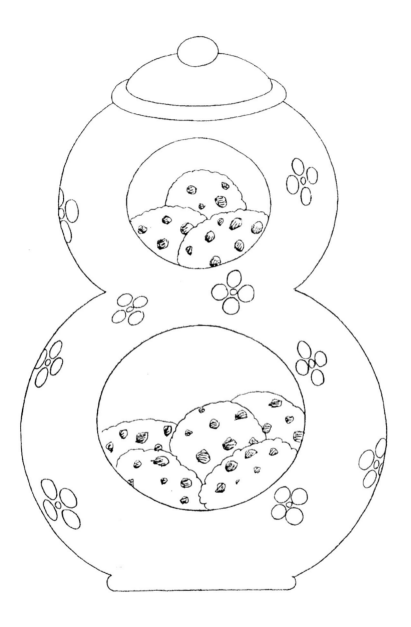

227

The Eighth Commandment

You Shall Not Steal

Here is one of my favorites, and a favorite of children too. The number 8 is a cookie jar. Don't steal!

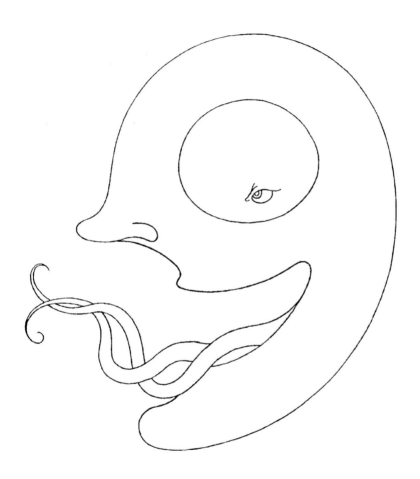

The Ninth Commandment

Do Not Bear False Witness
or
"Don't Lie"

Bearing false witness in the context of court is a pretty complicated concept for children, but they can easily learn the corollary, don't lie.

In this picture, the number 9 has been turned into a snake-like beast with a forked tongue. The Native American Indians used to say, "The white man speaks with forked tongue," because promises were always being made and broken.

The Tenth Commandment

You Shall Not Covet
or
"Put God First, Others Second, And Me Last"

Covet is a tough word for children. But when you teach them the word wrapped around the concept of putting God first, others second and themselves last, they get it! Be sure and teach them both the word covet and the phrase that explains it.

Appendix Two

Suggested Reading

There have been five books that have changed my life. One of them is Ray Sutton's *That You May Prosper,* which is an outstanding study of the biblical model for covenant, and whose influence you will have read on practically every page of this book.

Joy Davidman's *Smoke on the Mountain,* written in 1953, is still, to me, one of the best books available on the Ten Commandments. While somewhat dated, the book rings true in our own time, and the conditions of society which she observed half a century ago have now grown up into the monsters she warned of.

There are two catechisms which are invaluable for insights into the Ten Commandments. The first, Martin Luther's *Small Catechism*, was originally published in 1529 and has stood the test of time for nearly 500 years. The second, *The Catechism of the Catholic Church*, was published in 1994. While serving as the official teaching of the Roman Catholic Church, it offers a wealth of data by which any Christian would be enriched.

About the Author

Kenneth Myers was born in 1959 in Denison, Texas. The son of a pastor/missionary, he married Shirley McSorley in 1977. They have three children and two grandchildren. He is an Anglican bishop and pastors Christ Church Cathedral in Sherman, Texas.

www.kennethmyers.net

CPSIA information can be obtained at www.ICGtesting.com
Printed in the USA
LVOW10s1317100614

389406LV00053B/941/P